UNDERSTANDING THE ENGLISH LEGAL SYSTEM

WITHDRAWN

I ⁻ MAY 1990   A

Cavendish
Publishing
Limited

London • Sydney

UNDERSTANDING THE ENGLISH LEGAL SYSTEM

DJ Gifford PhD (Cantab)
Associate Professor in Law at the University of Queensland, Australia
Sometime WM Tapp Research Student, Gonville and Caius College
University of Cambridge

and

John R Salter MA (Oxon)
Solicitor
Visiting Professor of Law at Cranfield University

Cavendish
Publishing
Limited

London • Sydney

First published in Great Britain 1997 by Cavendish Publishing Limited, The Glass House, Wharton Street, London WC1X 9PX.

Telephone: 0171-278 8000   Facsimile: 0171-278 8080

E-mail: info@cavendishpublishing.com

Visit our Home Page on http://www.cavendishpublishing.com

Gifford, Donald
Understanding the English legal system.
1. Law – Great Britain
I. Title II. Salter, John
344.1

ISBN 1 85941 239 4

Printed and bound in Great Britain

THE PURPOSE OF THIS BOOK

What is it that constitutes our law? Which are the institutions that enable our legal system to operate? Can our law and its legal system be improved? How does our law apply, and how does it operate? The answers to these questions are of vital importance.

For whom are those answers vitally important? They are important for:

- law students;
- students in a wide range of studies including politics, environment, accountancy, commerce, engineering, and many others;
- officers entering the civil service;
- chief executive officers and managers, in statutory bodies, commerce, and industry;
- persons starting a career in management;
- persons running their own small business;
- and generally anyone interested in learning about the system of law and government under which we live and work.

It is the purpose of this book to set out in plain language what such an enquirer needs to know about the law, its institutions, and its operation. It is also the purpose of this book to draw attention to some of the areas in which the law needs to be improved or revised to meet the changing needs of the community, and to discuss why there is that need and how best it may be met.

Part 2 outlines the nature and operation of legal aid.

Part 3 is designed to give the reader an appreciation of the European Community bodies and documents that have an impact, often an important impact, on our British legal system.

D J Gifford

CONTENTS

The Purpose of This Book ... *v*

Table of Cases ... *xv*

Table of Statutes ... *xix*

Table of Statutory Instruments ... *xxi*

Glossary ... *xxiii*

PART 1 HOW TO UNDERSTAND OUR ENGLISH LEGAL SYSTEM

1 THE NATURE OF OUR LAW ... 3
A test of law ... 3
Rules outside the legal system ... 3
The problem of enforcement ... 4

2 THE SOURCES OF OUR LAW ... 5
The five sources of our law ... 5
Common law ... 5
Statute law ... 8
Subordinate legislation ... 9
Custom ... 10

3 FINDING THE LAW ... 11
Common law ... 11
Statute law ... 12
Subordinate legislation ... 12
Custom ... 12

4 THE PARLIAMENTARY SYSTEM ... 13
The origins of Parliament ... 13
The two-House system ... 13
Secretaries of State and ministers ... 13
The Cabinet system ... 13
Parliamentary committees ... 14
The Crown ... 14
Sovereignty ... 15

5 THE MAKING OF LAW BY PARLIAMENT ... 17
Origins of statutes ... 17
The minimal role of electors in the making of law by Parliament ... 18
The drafting of an Act of Parliament ... 19
The role of the governing parliamentary party ... 19
The role of the House of Lords ... 20
The role of Cabinet ... 21
The parliamentary procedure for making an Act of Parliament ... 21

The timing of a Bill   21
Procedure after enactment   22

6 INTERPRETING AN ACT OF PARLIAMENT   23

The need for statutes to be interpreted   23
Imperfections in the use of language   24
The fact that words do not have a single universally accepted meaning   24
Inadequacies in the instructions given   25
Failure to foresee changed circumstances   25
Failure to revise the legislation   26
Lack of technical knowledge   26
Insufficient knowledge   26
Drafting in urgency   26
Several Acts dealing with the same subject matter   26
Failure to consider other provisions of the same Act   27
Failure to use the same word in the same sense throughout   27
Overlooking a statutory definition   27
Amendments that are made in a statute other than the statute
  being amended   27
Legislation in general terms has to be applied to specific circumstances   28
Absurdity or injustice   28
The role of statutory interpretation   30
The rules of statutory interpretation   30

7 SUBORDINATE LEGISLATION   33

The nature of subordinate legislation   33
The way in which power is delegated   33
The authorities to which power is commonly delegated   33
The reasons for delegation   33
Advantages of delegation   34
Disadvantages of delegation   34
Court supervision of subordinate legislation   35

8 HOW JUDGES DEVELOP THE LAW   37

The hierarchy of the courts   37
Development of the law by tribunals and by courts of less than
  superior court status   37
Development of the law by courts of superior court status   38
The doctrine of precedent   38
The basis of the doctrine of precedent   38
The extent to which a decision constitutes a precedent   39
Whether a court is bound by its own previous decisions   39
How a court uses a precedent   39
Precedent as restricting the development of the legal system   41

Precedent as developing the law 42
Some major areas of development of the law through precedent 43

9 HOW EFFECTIVE IS OUR LAW-MAKING PROCESS? 45
Parliament 45
Courts 46
The effectiveness of the law-making process as a whole 47

10 THE LEGAL PROFESSION 49
Solicitors 49
Barristers 49
Queen's Counsel 49
Specialisation 49

11 THE HANDLING OF DISPUTES WITHIN THE LEGAL SYSTEM 51
How disputes can arise 51
Disposing of a dispute without a court decision 52
Judges, magistrates, and justices 54
The jurisdiction of the courts 54
Disposing of a civil dispute by judicial decision 55

12 THE TRIAL OF A CIVIL CASE 57
Pleadings 57
Interrogatories 58
Discovery 58
Interlocutory proceedings 59
Representation of the parties 59
The hearing 59
The standard of proof in a civil case 61
The decision 61
Enforcement of the decision in a civil case 61

13 THE TRIAL OF A CRIMINAL CASE 63
Is what has occurred a crime? 63
Investigation of offences 64
The extent to which an individual is obliged to answer police questions 64
The right to prosecute 65
The right to a fair trial 65
Bail and remand 65
Summary trial 66
The rule against double jeopardy 66
Representation 67
Selecting a jury 67

Procedure at the trial   67
Deciding the facts and the law   68

14 THE ADVERSARY SYSTEM   69
The meaning of the adversary system   69
The advantages of the adversary system   69
Disadvantages of the adversary system   70
Attempts to exclude the legal profession   71

15 THE RULES OF EVIDENCE   73
The meaning of evidence   73
The different types of evidence   73
The purpose of the rules of evidence   74
The exclusion of inadmissible evidence   74
Evaluating evidence   75
Circumstantial evidence   75
Prima facie evidence   76
Hearsay evidence   76
Judicial notice   76
Presumption of accuracy   76
Refreshing a witness's memory   76
Without prejudice letters or conversations   77
Admissions   77

16 THE JURY SYSTEM   79
The origin of the jury system   79
The function of the jury   79
Justification for retaining juries in criminal trials   79
Justification for retaining juries in civil cases   80
Criticisms of juries in criminal cases   80
Criticisms of juries in civil cases   81
Extension or restriction of the use of juries in criminal cases   81
Jury reforms   82

17 THE PUNISHMENT OF OFFENDERS   85
The principal purposes of the criminal law   85
The purposes of punishment   87
Capital punishment   88
Imprisonment   88
Psychiatric treatment during imprisonment   89
Work release   90
Periodic detention   90
Work orders   90

Youth training centres   91
Corporal punishment   91
Fine   91
Suspended sentence   92
Bond   92
Adjournment   92
Parole   93
Probation   93
The punishment of juvenile offenders   93
The difficulty of sentencing   93
The changing approach to punishment   94

18 THE INEVITABILITY OF LIMITATIONS   95
Human frailties within the legal system   95
Conflicting needs of perfection, certainty and speed   98
The importance of knowing the limitations of the legal system   99

19 LIMITATIONS ON THE EFFECTIVENESS OF PARLIAMENT   101
The purpose of Parliament   101
Limitations on the choice of members of the House of Commons   101
Limitations on representation of sections of the community   102
Limitations on the power of private members   103
Limitations on Parliament's responsiveness to changes in the electorates   104
Limitations on Parliament as a law-making body   105
Parliament's sources of information   106

20 LIMITATIONS ON THE EFFECTIVENESS OF SUBORDINATE LAW-MAKING BODIES   107
The nature of subordinate law-making bodies   107
Difficulties in producing effective subordinate legislation   107

21 LIMITATIONS ON THE EFFECTIVENESS OF THE COURTS   109
Lack of knowledge of legal rights   109
Lack of preparedness to use the court system   110
Limitations arising from the cost of litigation   110
Limitations caused by delay   111
Speedy hearings in urgent cases   113
Unavailability of the court system   113

22 LIMITATIONS ON THE EFFECTIVENESS OF THE COMMON LAW   115
The courts rely on the litigant   115
Common law principles affected by statute   115
Conservatism on the Bench   116

23 LIMITATIONS ON THE ENFORCEMENT OF LAW 119
Lack of community knowledge of the law 119
Lack of community acceptance of particular laws 119
Limited detection of offences and offenders 120
Government as protecting itself from the law 120

24 THE CHANGING ROLE OF THE LEGAL PROFESSION 123
Attempts to exclude lawyers 123
Attempts to exclude the courts 123
The extension of the legal profession into new fields 124

25 CHANGE AND THE LAW 127
The law has always been changing 127
The general acceptability of our legal system 127
The comparative effectiveness of various methods of changing the law 128

PART 2 HOW TO UNDERSTAND LEGAL AID

26 LEGAL AID 135
What legal aid is 135
Types of legal aid 135
The Legal Aid Board 135
Informative brochures 135
The financial criteria test 136
Applications for European legal aid 136
Proposed change to the system 136

PART 3 HOW TO UNDERSTAND THE IMPACT OF ASPECTS OF THE EUROPEAN COMMUNITY LEGAL SYSTEM ON OUR ENGLISH LEGAL SYSTEM

27 THE DIFFERENT BASES OF BRITISH AND OF EUROPEAN COMMUNITY LEGAL SYSTEMS 139
Court systems 139
Treaties as the basis of European Community law 139
Subordinate legislation 140
Points of conflict 141

28 THE BASIC TREATIES 143
The basic European Community Treaties 143
The Treaty of Rome 143
Treaty-based policies 143
European Community economic policies – coal and steel 143
European Community nuclear policy 144

29 EUROPEAN COMMUNITY INSTITUTIONS 145
Mergers under the Treaty of Rome 145
The Community institutions 145
The impact of European Community institutions on British law 146
The Council of the European Community Union 146
The European Parliament 147
The European Commission 148
The Court of Auditors 148
The European Court of Justice 148

**30 THE EFFECT OF THE EUROPEAN COMMUNITY
    LEGAL SYSTEM ON BRITAIN** 149
Effect on the British Parliament 149
Effect on the British courts 149

31 NOW READ ON 153
Further reading 153
Textbook on the English system 153
Textbooks on the European Community system 153

Index *155*

TABLE OF CASES

Attorney General (Canada) v Hallett & Carey Ltd [1952] AC 427 29

Bass Charrington (North) Ltd v Minister of Housing and
    Local Government (1970) 22 P&CR 31 52
Bristol District Council v Clark [1975] 1 WLR 1443 35
British Railways Board v Herrington [1972] AC 877 116
Bulmer (HP) Ltd v J Bollinger SA [1974] 2 All ER 1226;
    [1974] 2 CMLR 91 140
Burnett v Great North of Scotland Railway Co (1885) 10 App Cas 147 43

Cambridge Water Co v Eastern Counties Leather plc [1994] 2 AC 264 7
Camden London Borough Council v Post Office [1977] 1 WLR 892 28
Caparo Industries plc v Dickman [1990] 2 AC 605 6
Chiffman v Order of St John [1936] 1 All ER 557 7
Chokolingo v Attorney General [1981] 1 WLR 106 29
Coleen Properties Ltd v Minister of Housing and Local
    Government [1971] 1 WLR 433 52
Collier v Nokes (1849) 2 Car & Kir 1012 76
Commission v Council [1987] (Case 45/86) ECR 1493 146
Commission v Spain [1993] (The Santona Marshes case)
    (Case C-355/90) 1 ECR 4221 150

Danielsson and Others v Commission (1995) (Case T-219/95)
    (unreported) 151
Donoghue v Stephenson [1932] AC 562 ....39, 40, 116

Eton College (Provost) v Great Western Railway Co
    (1839) 1 Ry and Can Cas 200 43

Glebe Sugar Refining Co v Trustees of the Port and
    Harbours of Greenock [1921] SC HL 72 69
Grant v Australian Knitting Mills [1936] AC 85 40
Groves v Wimborne [1898] 2 QB 402 42

HKJ (an infant), Re [1967] 2 QB 617 8
Hale v Jennings Brothers [1938] 1 All ER 579 7

Income Tax Special Purposes Commissioners v Pemsel [1891] AC 531 24
Imperial Tobacco Ltd v Attorney General [1981] AC 718 97
India, The (No 2) (1984) 33 LJPN&A 193 4

Kruse v Johnson [1892] 2 QB 91 35
Kurama v The Queen [1955] AC 197 64

Lemmon v Webb [1895] AC 1 53

Litster v Forth Dry Dock & Engineering Company
Limited [1990] AC 546, HL 150

Loweth v Minister of Housing and Local Government
(1970) 22 P&CR 125 52

Mersey Docks & Harbour Board v Henderson (1888) 13 App Cas 29

Milch-, Fett- und Eirkontor GmbH v Hauptzollamt
SaarbrŸcken [1969] (Case 29/68) ECR 165..8, 139

Millar v Taylor (1769) 4 Burr 2303 30

Muras v Hauptzollamt Hamburg-Jonas [1973] (Case 12/73) ECR 963 141

Nairn v University of St Andrews [1909] AC 147...30

Parker v British Airways Board [1982] QB 1004 ....5, 46

Pepper v Hart [1993] AC 593...30

Pickstone v Freemans plc [1989] AC 66, HL..150

Pretura Unificata di Torino v Persons Unknown [1988]
(Case 228/87) ECR 5099 151

Priestly v Fowler (1837) 3 M&W 1 41

Punjab National Bank v Boinville [1992] 1 WLR 1138 6

R v Arrowsmith [1975] 1 All ER 463..65

R v Darby [1980] 2 All ER 166; [1980] 2 WLR 597; [1980] 2 CMLR 229 149

R v Deputy Governor of Parkhurst Prison, ex p Hague
[1990] 3 WLR 1210 114

R v Liverpool Corporation, ex p Liverpool Taxi Fleet
Operators' Association [1972] 2 QB 299, CA..8

R v London County Council, ex p The Entertainment
Protection Association Ltd [1932] 2 KB 215 4

R v Osbourne [1973] 1 QB 678..73

R v Secretary of State for the Environment, ex p The Royal
Society for the Protection of Birds (1995) The Times, 10 February.................150

R v Secretary of State for Foreign and Commonwealth Affairs,
ex p Indian Association of Alberta [1982] QB 892...10

Ridge v Baldwin [1964] AC 40, HL...8

Rylands v Fletcher (1868) LR 3 HL 330..7

Sankey v Whitlam (1978) 142 CLR 1 97

Seven Bishops' case (1688) 12 State Tr 183...79

Sumner v William Henderson & Sons [1963] 1 WLR 823 115

Sutherland Shire Council v Heyman (1985) 157 CLR 424.....................................6

Taylor v National Assistance Board [1957] P 101; [1958] AC 532 29

Thames Guaranty Ltd v Campbell [1985] QB 210 112
Tito v Waddell (No 2) [1977] Ch 106 15

Victoria Square Property Co Ltd v Southwark London
  Borough Council [1978] 1 WLR 463..52
Videan v British Transport Commission [1963] 2 QB 650 116

Warre's Will Trusts, Re [1953] 2 All ER 99 24
Wood v Blair & Helmsley Rural District Council (1957) 4 ALR 243 ....43, 115

Zanetti (R) and Others [1990] (Case C-359/88) ECR 1509...152

TABLE OF STATUTES

Acquisition of Land Act 1981 109

Act of Accession 1972 141

Agricultural Holdings Act 1948
  s 9 28

Clean Air Act 1993
  Sched 6 28

Consumer Credit Act 1974 28

Criminal Justice Act 1988 67

Environment Act 1995 87
  s 114 123
  Sched 20 123

Environmental Protection Act 1990
  Sched 3 28

Equal Pay Act 1970
  s 1(2)(c) 150

European Communities Act 1972 140
  Part I 141

Housing Act 1985 .... 9, 27
  s 23(1) 28
  s 579(1) 109
  s 621 27
  s 622 27
  s 623 27

Interpretation Act 1889 27

Interpretation Act 1978 27

Leasehold Reform, Housing and
  Urban Development Act 1993
  Sched 21 28

Legal Aid Act 1988 135
  Part V 135
  s 19 135

Libel Act 1792 96

Local Government, Planning
  and Land Act 1980
  s 4(4)(e) 109

National Heritage Act 1983 28

Noise and Statutory Nuisance
  Act 1993
  s 4 28

Representation of the People
  Act 1985 9

Restrictive Trade Practices
  Act 1976 87

Restrictive Trade Practices
  Act 1977 87

Single European Act 1986 .... 140, 143, 145

Town and Country Planning
  Act 1971 123

Transport Act
  Sched 8 109

Witchcraft Act 1735 18

TABLE OF STATUTORY INSTRUMENTS

Legal Aid Advice and Assistance (Scope)
Regulations 1989 (SI 1989/550) 135
Legal Aid in Criminal and Care Proceedings (General)
Regulations 1989 (SI 1989/344) 135

GLOSSARY

Act   a law which has been made by Parliament – an Act of Parliament (also called a statute)

Assent   the approval given to an Act of Parliament by the reigning King or Queen

Bill   the draft of a proposed Act of Parliament (the term 'Bill' is used to describe the draft before Parliament has passed it and it receives the royal assent as an Act)

Enactment   an Act

Hansard   The publication in which are recorded the speeches made in Parliament

Legislation   law made by a body which has power to make law – the term is often used to refer to law made by persons or bodies whose law-making powers are given to them by Act of Parliament

Precedent   a decision by the High Court of Justice or by the Court of Appeal, the House of Lords or the Privy Council

Statute   another name for an Act of Parliament

Subordinate legislation   a law which is made by some person or body other than Parliament and acting under the authority of an Act of Parliament

PART 1

HOW TO UNDERSTAND OUR ENGLISH LEGAL SYSTEM

CHAPTER 1

THE NATURE OF OUR LAW

A test of law

Law is an officially recognised, enforceable system of rules. There are many rules in our society which are not officially recognised, and which do not therefore constitute law. For example, within a family there are many rules which are in practice binding on the family members but which are not enforceable as laws. The child who breaks those rules may suffer punishment; but, however just that punishment may be, it is not punishment as part of the legal system. The law intervenes only in cases in which the punishment inflicted amounts to maltreatment of the child.

Rules outside the legal system

Rules of law may be made by Parliament or by statutory bodies authorised by Parliament to exercise law-making powers. Law-making powers may also be conferred on individuals in public office such as the Secretary of State for the Environment or the Secretary of State for Transport. Judges of the High Court of Justice or of higher courts interpret the law, and the law they have developed over the centuries on a case-by-case basis is no less part of the law than the law contained in Acts of Parliament.

There are, however, other rules that are not part of our law. A cricketer may be declared out by an umpire exercising a power conferred by cricketing rules: the umpire may have misinterpreted one of the cricketing rules; but, as those are not part of the law of England (as distinct from the rules of the International Cricket Council) the cricketer cannot rush to a judge for an order that his innings be reinstated.

In a different category again are rules made by unincorporated clubs, societies, and associations. Their rules are made and changed by their members. They are not part of our law. They can be enforced, not as law, but because they form a contract between all the members. Such a club may be a tennis club, a political association, or a club to foster some particular hobby (to cite a few examples). The rules of such clubs (unless they are charities or friendly societies) do not have to be registered with any official body; they are made by the members, and they do not form part of the law of the land. Nevertheless, members may enforce the rules as against other members or against the club committee on the basis that those rules form a contract between all the members.

The rules so far considered are not made by the community as such, although the community, through its legal system, may be prepared to enforce them. Rules of this nature are to be contrasted with law properly so-called, which consists of rules made by the community through Parliament, through bodies authorised by Parliament, through the courts, or by custom. Laws of this kind bind the citizen regardless of whether or not that person as an individual agrees to them and regardless of whether or not that person considers them desirable. Such laws apply even to the temporary visitor to a country, who of course has no vote and has no say in the content of the laws. A good example is provided by the law of Saudi Arabia which provides for a flogging as the punishment for drinking or providing alcohol – punishment which has been inflicted upon foreigners who have committed that offence within Saudi Arabia even although it is not against their religion or customs to drink alcohol and it is not a breach of the laws of their own country.

The problem of enforcement

Enforceability of the law has always been a problem. In a developed society such as our own it is customary to think of the enforcement of the law in terms of enforcement by the police, or by departmental officers, or by officers of local government authorities. However, although it is of the essence of law that it is enforceable, that enforcement need not be by the State as such. Unless Parliament has prohibited it or required the consent of the Attorney General to be first obtained in respect of the relevant criminal offences, there is still a right in a private person to institute a prosecution for breach of the criminal law.

Although the law has to be enforceable, this does not necessarily mean that every law in a particular country is always enforced. Enforcement as distinct from enforceability is not a test of what is law. Even the fact that a particular law has not been enforced for a long period does not destroy its nature as 'law'. As Dr Lushington said:

> No doubt exists that a British Act of Parliament does not become inoperative by mere non-use, however long the time may have been since it was known to have been actually put in force.[1]

In a case before the Court of Appeal Scrutton LJ said:

> So long as an Act is on the statute book, the way to get rid of it is to repeal or alter it in Parliament, not for subordinate bodies, who are bound to obey the law, to take it upon themselves to disobey an Act of Parliament.[2]

---

1   *The India (No 2)* (1984) 33 LJPN&A 193.
2   *R v London County Council ex p The Entertainment Protection Association Ltd* [1931] 2 KB 215 at 226.

CHAPTER 2

THE SOURCES OF OUR LAW

The five sources of our law

Law as we know it today derives from five sources: common law, statute law, subordinate legislation, custom, and European Community law. These five sources of law are very different in their nature, and it is necessary to consider each one separately.[1]

Common law

Common law is the law as developed through the decisions of the judges. Its rules are developed through a series of cases decided by various judges over a period of years. Sometimes this period may be fairly short when the law is developing rapidly; at other times development may take centuries. What constitutes the common law is not so much the actual decision in a particular case as the principles upon which that decision is based. Whilst some cases are of course of very great importance, it is normal for a principle of the common law to be enunciated in a series of cases in the same field. Each case helps to develop the principle a little further. This has been explained by Donaldson LJ (later Lord Donaldson of Lymington MR) who said that the judges:

> have both the right and the duty to extend and adapt the common law in the light of established principles and the current needs of the community. This is not to say that we start with a clean sheet. In doing so, we should draw from the experience of the past as revealed by the previous decisions of the courts.[2]

The difference between a decision on the one hand, and the principles on which that decision is based on the other hand, can be clearly seen by considering the case in which one motorist sues another for damages resulting from a motor accident, a very common form of litigation today. The fact that a particular judge awards a particular sum as the amount to be paid by a particular motorist by way of damages for a particular accident does not establish any principle, and it therefore does not form part of the common law. However, if the judge arrives at the decision as to which (or both) of the parties is negligent and as to the extent of that negligence by the application of a principle, that principle does form part of the common law.

In deciding what does or does not form part of the common law it is necessary to have regard to the status of the court making the particular decision. Not only is there the distinction between the decision in the particular case and the principles upon which that decision is based, but there is also a distinction between the various levels of court within the hierarchy of courts. From the level of justices of the peace sitting as a panel or the stipendiary magistrate sitting alone, the hierarchy proceeds upwards through a series of courts, some of which can and others of which cannot contribute to the common

---

1   European Community Law is considered in Part 3 of this book.
2   *Parker v British Airways Board* [1982] QB 1004 at 1008.

law. The distinction between the courts which can contribute to the common law and those which cannot does not even depend upon whether the presiding officer of the court has the status of a judge. For example, a county court is presided over by a judge; yet the principles enunciated in that judge's decisions are not treated as contributing to the common law. The reason for this is that it is only those courts of superior court status from which the common law is derived. The superior courts start upwards from the High Court of Justice (a court divided into divisions, the best known of which is the Queen's Bench Division) through the Court of Appeal to the House of Lords.

The concept of a superior court is also used in various countries using the common law system, and on rare but increasing occasions English courts have drawn upon such decisions. Both the Court of Appeal[3] and the House of Lords[4] have found it appropriate to rest a decision upon such a case.

Not all decisions of the superior courts contribute to the common law. There are many decisions which depend upon their own facts and contain no new statement of principle and, for that matter, no new development of an existing principle. Those decisions, of course, cannot contribute to the common law. The decisions of the superior courts are considered by experienced members of the legal profession who decide whether or not particular decisions should be published as contributing to the development of the common law. Those decisions are published in series of books known as law reports.

Law reports have existed for many centuries, the earliest being the *Year Books*, which go back to the reign of Edward II: the earliest copies of the *Year Books* in fact go back to 1290.

The person untrained in law who goes to a public library or a law library in search of the law may be misled by the fact that there are series of reports of courts below the status of superior courts, and even series of reports of tribunals. An example is the series of reports published under the name *Planning Appeal Decisions*[5] and recording decisions by departmental inspectors, occasionally by Queen's Counsel, and in the more important cases by the Secretary of State for the Environment. Those reports are important to lawyers appearing before those courts or before those tribunals. Just as the decisions of the superior courts contain principles of the common law, so the decisions of specialised courts and tribunals contain principles which those courts or tribunals will apply in later cases; but that does not give the court or tribunal the status of a superior court, and so it does not make its decisions part of the common law.

The fact that it is the judges, and the judges alone, who make the common law can be clearly seen by considering the position of a legal textbook. There are

---

3   *Punjab National Bank v de Boinville* [1992] 1 WLR 1138, applying the reasons for a decision of Brennan J (later Brennan CJ) in *Sutherland Shire Council v Heyman* (1985) 157 CLR 424 at 481 (High Court of Australia).

4   *Caparo Industries plc v Dickman* [1990] 2 AC 605, also applying the reasons for decision of Brennan J (later Brennan CJ) in *Sutherland Shire Council v Heyman* (1985) 157 CLR 424 at 481 (High Court of Australia).

5   Published by Sweet & Maxwell.

many legal textbooks that are very detailed indeed. Some of those textbooks extend through a number of volumes in their consideration of a single topic of law. No matter how experienced and how highly regarded the author, however, the textbook itself does not form part of the common law. That that is so does not even depend upon the status of the author of that textbook. Even if the author is a judge of a superior court, the textbook does not form part of the common law. For example, Salmond J was a judge of the Supreme Court (now the High Court) of New Zealand: the principles which he set out in his judgments as a judge of that court did form part of the common law, but what he set out in his very highly regarded textbook was not part of the common law. Of course, if he expressed some view in his textbook and subsequently adopted and stated that view in a court judgment, it then became part of the common law because it was part of the reasons for the decision in that court.

The common law has a remarkable aptitude for flexibility. It would have been easy for the courts to adopt a restrictive approach to the contribution of each decision to the development of the common law. For example, the leading case of *Rylands v Fletcher*[6] was a decision of the House of Lords (sitting, of course, as the highest court in England) that, if water escaped from a landowner's dam and damaged a neighbour's land, that neighbour could sue for damages. The principle upon which that decision was based, however, has been applied in many different circumstances. For example, the principle in *Rylands v Fletcher* has been applied to a case in which the defect was not in the retaining wall of a dam but in the retaining cable of a form of merry-go-round (the particular machine had pseudo-aeroplanes in which the patrons sat and which were attached to the top of the machine by metal cables, these 'aeroplanes' flying out to the extent of the cable as the machine revolved). Unfortunately for the proprietor of the machine, one of the cables broke with the result that the 'aeroplane' flew further than intended and struck a bystander. The proprietor of the 'chair-O-plane' machine was held liable in damages to the bystander: *Hale v Jennings Brothers*.[7] Another case in which the principle in *Rylands v Fletcher* was applied concerned the well known St John Ambulance Society, that Society having erected a flagpole to mark the presence of its tent at a public function. When children played on the guyropes, the flagpole collapsed and struck a bystander: the application of the principle in *Rylands v Fletcher* resulted in the Society being held liable in damages to the bystander: *Chiffman v Order of St John*.[8]

It is that flexibility of the common law and the ability of its judges to apply its principles to changing circumstances that is its strength. It means that the common law can change and adapt to meet the changing needs of a rapidly changing community. When bureaucracy was only a minor factor of life, the common law found it unnecessary to concern itself much with it. Today, with the very rapid growth of bureaucratic institutions, the common law has developed a whole series of principles to regulate and control bureaucratic

---

6   (1868) LR 3 HL 330.

7   [1938] 1 All ER 579.

8   [1936] 1 All ER 557 (note that the scope of *Rylands v Fletcher* has more recently been limited by the House of Lords: *Cambridge Water Co v Eastern Counties Leather plc* [1994] 2 AC 264).

action. The principles so developed include widening the requirements of compliance with the rules of natural justice,[9] the development of a new requirement of fairness,[10] and a doctrine enabling the courts to give legal effect to legitimate expectations,[11] a concept well known to European Community law. Such flexibility allows judges to interpret English law so that it is not in conflict with European Community law. However, if a reference to the European Court of Justice is unavoidable, an interpretation of a provision of Community law given by the European Court by way of a preliminary ruling binds the national court making the reference.[12]

Of course, the common law is not a code. Indeed, its strength lies in the fact that it is not a code, for a code has an inbuilt rigidity. Nevertheless, the fact that the common law does develop, and necessarily develops, through the decisions in the individual cases – often over a long period – has been the subject of trenchant criticism. For example, Alfred, Lord Tennyson wrote in *Aylmer's Field*:

Mastering the lawless science of our law,
That codeless myriad of precedent,
That wilderness of single instances,
Through which a few, by wit or fortune led,
May beat a pathway out to wealth and fame.

Certainly, the common law can lack comprehensiveness in particular fields, and the state of its development at any particular time may depend upon the extent to which persons have been prepared to litigate upon particular topics. Yet that fact of itself reflects the importance of those topics to the public, for it is only on matters of importance to them that people ordinarily litigate, at least in the civil courts. Common law is by far the most prolific source of law.

Statute law

Statute law is very prominent in the public mind; but, despite the large number of new statutes produced in recent years, statute law still takes third place after common law and subordinate legislation as a source of legal rules. Statute law is law produced by Act of Parliament. The terms 'Act of Parliament' and 'statute law' are interchangeable.

Statute law is made by Parliament itself. An Act of Parliament does not have birth in the deciding of a particular case, but in the decision, for example, of a Secretary of State or minister, or of the Cabinet, or even of a private member of Parliament, that a new Act is needed. The intended Act has to pass through 'readings' in each House of Parliament and then receive the assent of the Queen before it becomes law.

Although the courts can develop the common law to meet the changing needs of the community, they can only do so as cases come before them. There

---

9   *Ridge v Baldwin* [1964] AC 40 (House of Lords).

10   *Re HKJ (an infant)* [1967] 2 QB 617 (Divisional Court).

11   *R v Liverpool Corporation ex p Liverpool Taxi Fleet Operators' Association* [1972] 2 QB 299 (Court of Appeal).

12   Case 29/68 *Milch-, Fett- und Eirkontor GmbH v Hauptzollamt Saarbrücken* [1969] ECR 165 at 179 and following.

might be an urgent need for a development of the law, and yet no case dealing with that aspect might come before a superior court at the time. Parliament can meet the need immediately by passing an Act. A comparatively early example of meeting a need immediately by the passing of a statute occurred in 1531 when the Bishop of Rochester's cook poisoned a vessel of yeast, causing a number of people to become ill and one to die. Henry VIII, whose love for food is still notorious, hurried an Act through Parliament providing for that cook, and any other poisoner, to be executed by being boiled to death.[13]

When a case does come before a superior court, that court can only deal with those aspects of the law involved in the case. It cannot lay down a comprehensive code of the type that can be set out in an Act. Many of the Acts are very detailed. The Housing Act 1985 has 625 sections and 24 schedules. There can also be a need for an Act if Parliament considers that the existing law is wrong, or if it considers that a court has wrongly decided what the law is and wants to substitute its own view of the law. The more complex society gets, the greater its need for statutes. As society gets more complex, new abuses develop, and society finds new subjects for control either in the interest of the State or of the individual.

Despite the fact that it only ranks third in volume as a source of law, the Act of Parliament is nevertheless a prolific source.

Subordinate legislation

Subordinate legislation is legislation made under the authority of an Act of Parliament. Originally when Parliament was making law upon a particular topic it set out the whole of the law it intended to make in the statute itself. As life has become more complex, and as the structure of government has grown and expanded, resort has been had to leaving the making of a great deal of the law to government departments and statutory authorities. In some instances, the major part of the law being made by Parliament is still to be found in the Act itself, with a power to make subordinate legislation being conferred to fill in the details. In other instances, however, the statute is a mere skeleton, by far the major part of the legislation on the topic being by way of subordinate legislation.

Subordinate legislation takes many forms. One form of subordinate legislation is that of regulations.[14] Another is an order made by the relevant Secretary of State or minister.[15] Another form is that of rules.[16] All three of those examples fall within the comprehensive term of statutory instruments. There is no magic to the particular form which subordinate legislation takes in a particular case.

---

13 Fay, *Discoveries in the Statute Book*, 1939, Sweet & Maxwell, at 77–78.

14 As an example, the Education (Mandatory Awards) Regulations 1985 when they came into force had 27 regulations with a total of 78 subregulations and five schedules.

15 An example is the Representation of the People Act 1985 (Commencement No 1) Order 1985.

16 An example is the Police Authorities (Appointment of Magistrates) (Metropolitan Counties and Northumbria Police Area) Rules 1985.

Subordinate legislation is an even more prolific source of law than statute, coming second in this respect after the common law. Subordinate legislation is not only very common, but individual pieces of subordinate legislation are amended very frequently. Today the bulk of subordinate legislation in any given year is several times as large as the volume of statute law produced in the same period.

Custom

Law established by custom was at its strongest in early forms of society. For example, speaking of the Canadian Indians, Lord Denning MR said:

> They had their chiefs and headmen to regulate their simple society and to enforce their customs. I say 'to enforce their customs', because in early societies custom is the basis of law. Once a custom is established it gives rise to rights and obligations which the chiefs and headmen will enforce. These customary laws are not written down. They are handed down by tradition from one generation to another. Yet beyond doubt they are well established and have the force of law within the community.[17]

In the early period of the common law custom was a very important source of legal rules. Many such rules were incorporated into the common law itself. The best example is the law merchant. Originally the law merchant was the custom of merchants, which in time became accepted by the judges as part of the common law. The modern law on sale of goods has grown far beyond the early customs of the medieval fairs, but the principles developed then and accepted by the common law still remain part of our law today.

At the present time custom as such plays very little part in the development of our law, partly because both the courts and Parliament are playing such a large role themselves that they do not wait for the law to be shaped by custom. The principal role of custom today is to be found in the law of meetings, some of the rules in this area still being rules of custom. However, custom can still be made today. In the second half of the 20th century the Court of Aldermen of the City of London started a new custom to be applied in determining whether an alderman is suitable to be elected as Aldermanic Sheriff of the City or to be elected as Lord Mayor. Twenty years later the custom was challenged. The challenge failed, the courts upholding the custom.

---

17 *R v Secretary of State for Foreign and Commonwealth Affairs ex p Indian Association of Alberta* [1982] QB 892 at 910.

CHAPTER 3

FINDING THE LAW

Common law

How we got Common Law .

The common law is to be found in the decisions of the judges of the superior courts. It might be thought that, being court decisions, they would be published by the courts themselves or at least by the government. In point of fact, however, they are not. They are published in series of volumes known as law reports. The earliest law reports (the *Year Books*) are of uncertain origin: some have thought that they were published by court officials at the expense of the Crown, but the generally accepted view today is that they were law students' notebooks. In 1875 the Incorporated Council of Law Reporting for England and Wales commenced publishing an official series of reports under the title *The Law Reports*. That series is still being published today. The annual bound volumes of *The Law Reports* provide separate volumes for the separate divisions of the High Court (including decisions of the Court of Appeal) and for the House of Lords in its judicial capacity. Additionally, the Incorporated Council publishes a weekly series entitled *The Weekly Law Reports* – a series that includes not only the decisions that will appear later in *The Law Reports* but also decisions that justify publication but are not included in *The Law Reports*. In addition to the two series produced by the Incorporated Council there is a series produced by a commercial publisher in respect of the very same courts and including many of the same decisions. The common law, therefore, is to be found both in the series of reports published by the Incorporated Council and in the series of reports published by commercial publishers.

Most law reports follow a particular style. They begin with the name of the court, the name of the case (the names of the parties), the judge's name, and the dates of hearing and of decision. Then come the 'catchwords', a series of brief phrases referring to the most important points decided in that case. After that comes the 'head note': this sets out the facts of the case and a brief summary of what was decided. It is usual then to set out the names of the lawyers who appeared in the case, and sometimes a summary of their argument. It is at this point that the judgment is set out.[1] The judgments normally make up the bulk of the report of any decision, and today almost invariably do so. The report ends with a summary of the order made and a statement of the names of the solicitors for the respective parties.

Volumes of law reports are appearing in considerable numbers every year. In a typical year (1987) *The Weekly Law Reports* contained 4381 pages and *The All England Law Reports* contained 3924 pages. To find these cases the lawyer uses *The Digest*[2] and *Halsbury's Laws of England*[3] but, as the one case may raise a number of points of law, the reader may have to turn to many pages of those

---

1   If the court comprises two or more judges there may be one judgment or several.
2   Butterworths, London.
3   Butterworths, London.

publications in the course of research on a particular case. To meet this problem various publishers provide law reports on computer disks – a service that is useful for lawyers but dangerous for the ordinary person who does not understand legal terminology and principles.

Statute law

There is a problem to ascertaining what Parliament has enacted upon any particular topic of law. This problem arises from the fact that Parliament frequently includes a number of topics in the one statute. The search for the statute law is made all the more difficult by the fact that there is no really effective index to it. Furthermore, lawyers and other people wishing to know the law contained in the statutes must look very carefully not only at the statute but also at the amendments which Parliament has made to it from time to time.

Subordinate legislation

Subordinate legislation is the second most prolific source of law. It is a confused mass, a maze in which even the experienced in the field can get lost.

Custom

The very nature of custom ensures that there can be no index to it. Anyone wishing to prove the existence of a custom has to do it by evidence before the court in the particular case.

CHAPTER 4

THE PARLIAMENTARY SYSTEM

The origins of Parliament

We have seen how the common law develops from case to case and how this incremental development has allowed the common law to reflect changing community needs and ethics.[1] Parliament, too, has developed incrementally. In our system Parliament (although with many differences from Parliament today) can be traced back to Simon de Montfort's Parliament of 1265. By the Model Parliament of 1295 Parliament was composed of the magnates[2] (in modern terminology the Lords), and representative knights, burgesses, and minor clergy,[3] and each of these groups had its deliberations separately from the others. By 1343 the number of meeting places had crystallised into two, one being that of the Lords lay and spiritual, the other being that of all other representatives. The two-House system had arrived.

The two-House system

Parliament as we know it today comprises two Houses – the House of Commons and the House of Lords. The House of Commons is composed of elected members. By contrast, the House of Lords comprises the hereditary peers, the bishops, the Law Lords,[4] and life peers appointed for their lifetime. The system under which Parliament consists of two Houses is known as the bicameral system.

Secretaries of State and ministers

At Parliamentary level administration of government is the responsibility of members of Parliament who hold office as a Secretary of State or a minister. It is usual for each Secretary of State and each minister to have the responsibility of supervising a government department or a statutory authority or of supervising two or more of them. Each Secretary of State and each minister is also responsible to Parliament for his or her actions or failures to act, and is also responsible for action or inaction on the part of any department or statutory authority within his or her portfolio.

The Cabinet system

A feature of parliamentary government is the existence of what is known as the Cabinet. The Cabinet is a group of Secretaries of State and of ministers in formal

---

1   See Common Law in Chapter 2.
2   The magnates comprised what are known today as the Lords lay and spiritual, those spiritual being the bishops.
3   By 1332 the lower clergy had ceased to be members of Parliament.
4   The Law Lords are eminent judges who are appointed to the House of Lords to discharge its duties as the ultimate appeal court.

meeting at which decisions are made upon questions of government policy and upon such matters as the substance of legislation to come before Parliament.

Although Parliament today functions on the party system, the Cabinet is not necessarily tied to it. For all practical purposes, it has for a long time been tied to the party system, save in times of national emergency: during the Napoleonic Wars there was the Cabinet known as the Ministry of All the Talents (a non-party Cabinet), and the Second World War saw a composite government of England composed of members of the major political parties, irrespective of the fact that one party had been elected as the government and the other lacked the numbers to form a government.

The number of ministers has led to an adaptation of the Cabinet system. There is now both a Cabinet and an inner Cabinet, the latter of course being more restricted in numbers and confined to the most senior of the Secretaries of State and ministers. The members of the inner Cabinet would be the Prime Minister, the Lord Chancellor, the deputy Prime Minister, the Chancellor of the Exchequer, and the remainder would ordinarily be Secretaries of State.

Parliamentary committees

An important feature of modern parliamentary government is the establishment of various committees. These committees are either standing committees or committees formed for a particular purpose and not intended to continue from Parliament to Parliament.

A parliamentary committee does not observe the rules of procedure that are observed in a court of law, and is not required to do so. Its members have many other commitments. They may find themselves unable to be present for particular parts of sittings of the committee or even for a whole sitting. That, in the case of a judge, would be unthinkable; but it is the system followed in respect of these committees composed of members with many other duties. A parliamentary committee does not legislate. It is not Parliament, but a committee of Parliament.

The Crown

The Crown is an institution quite separate from the Queen and also separate from Parliament. The ordinary person in the street tends to think of the Crown and the Queen as being one and the same, but in legal theory this is not so. Government buildings may still have the royal cipher, and judges still sit under the royal coat of arms; but the buildings are not owned by the Queen, and judges are appointed not by her personally but by the Lord Chancellor. By contrast, properties such as Sandringham Castle were bought by the monarch personally and not in the name of the Crown. There are many functions performed by the Queen personally. Some, such as entertaining the leader of another country, are well known to the public, although it is probably not widely realised that that function gives her the opportunity of influencing such a leader on important matters.

Another function is the appointment of a Prime Minister personally by the reigning sovereign. There is an interesting account by Winston Churchill of his appointment by King George VI as Prime Minister:

> I was taken immediately to the King. His Majesty received me most graciously and bade me sit down. He looked at me searchingly and quizzically for some moments, and then said: 'I suppose you don't know why I have sent for you?' Adopting his mood, I replied: 'Sir, I simply couldn't imagine why'. He laughed and said: 'I want to ask you to form a government'. I said I would certainly do so.[5]

A widely known function performed by the Queen personally is the delivery of the Queen's Speech. The speech is in fact prepared by the government and outlines the legislation expected to be brought before Parliament in the then current sessions. Members of the Commons (so far as space permits) assemble with the Lords in the House of Lords to hear the speech. No statute is valid until it has received the royal assent. Refusal of assent by the reigning monarch occurred during the reign of Queen Anne. King George III threatened to use his power of refusal but in the end did not have to exercise that power because the Prime Minister gave way.

The concept of the Crown is not limited to England. There are of course other countries independent of England but owing allegiance to the sovereign. For example, the concept applies in Australia, Canada, and New Zealand. In such a country a reference to the Crown means not the government of the United Kingdom but the government of the country concerned (or of a State or Province within that country). As Megarry V-C observed: 'It seems that at any rate for some purposes there are today as many Crowns as there are independent realms.'[6]

Sovereignty

The Parliament of the United Kingdom is sovereign. Within the United Kingdom it could make any laws it pleased. This position has been altered in recent years by Britain's membership of the European Community: British legislation can now be challenged, for example, under the Treaty of Rome, for so long as Britain remains a member of the European Community. Britain is also required to legislate to comply with the multitudinous directives issued by the European Community.

---

5   Churchill, Winston S (later Sir Winston Churchill), *The Second World War*, 1948, Cassell & Co Ltd, London, Vol I, at 525.
6   *Tito v Waddell (No 2)* [1977] Ch 106 at 231.

CHAPTER 5

THE MAKING OF LAW BY PARLIAMENT

Origins of statutes

A statute seldom, if ever, originates in Parliament. Its origins must be sought elsewhere. Many statutes owe their origin to a decision made by the officers of a government department that a law needs to be introduced to deal with a particular topic. A government department may decide new legislation is needed either to amend an existing Act, or to consolidate a number of Acts, or to introduce something new. Departments have first-hand experience of the working out of the legislation they administer, and that experience qualifies them to propose new law. A department's proposals are put up through its Secretary of State or its minister to Cabinet. If the departmental head convinces the Secretary of State or the minister responsible for that department, and if the Secretary of State or the minister convinces Cabinet, an Act may be passed. A semi-government body plays the same role in relation to its proposals for legislation that a department does for its.

Government policy is, of course, one of the origins of an Act of Parliament. Government policy may originate in a decision by the controlling body of the party in power in Parliament, or it may originate in what is referred to as the party room (the room in which the members of Parliament who belong to the political party in power at the time hold their meetings for party purposes), or it may originate at a Cabinet meeting. Government policy may also find its origin not in the policy of the British government but in the policy of one of the organs of the European Community.

Another source of a new statute is an agreement between the government and a company providing for special legislation to give agreed advantages to the company to induce it to locate in the United Kingdom or in some specified part of the United Kingdom. Local government also plays a part in causing draft legislation to be brought before Parliament. Trade associations, environmental groups and other active bodies lobby Secretaries of State, ministers, and other members of Parliament to try to achieve legislation, or legislation in a particular form, or to have an existing Act amended or repealed.

'Lobbying' is the term used for making representations at political level either to members of Parliament of the party in power, or to members of Parliament in the opposition or other parties, or to all of them. It is called 'lobbying' from the days when these representations were made in the lobbies of the House, as indeed many still are. There are persons who specialise in lobbying, that is who make it their paid occupation to make representations in this way on behalf of their clients. A particular industry, for example, may desire to make representations for the removal or reduction of an excise or VAT, or against its increase; and it may employ a professional lobbyist to make those representations for it. The media (newspapers, journals, radio and television stations) play a considerable part in bringing the idea of new legislation strongly to Parliament's attention. Judicial decisions may reveal a weakness in the law, and from time to time judges in the course of their decisions do expressly draw Parliament's attention to the need to remedy a defect.

Many statutes are outmoded or ineffective. The repeal of the Witchcraft Act by the Churchill government in England in 1944 is an example of legislation brought about to revise the law which had proved to be outmoded. It is interesting to read the note Winston Churchill wrote as Prime Minister to the Home Secretary on 3 April 1944 about a prosecution under that Act:

> Let me have a report on why the Witchcraft Act 1735 was used in a modern court of justice.

> What was the cost of this trial to the State – observing that witnesses were brought from Portsmouth and maintained here in this crowded London for a fortnight, and the Recorder kept busy with all this obsolete tomfoolery, to the detriment of necessary work in the courts.[1]

It is not uncommon for a government to appoint a commission, board or committee to enquire and report to it. Such a report may recommend new legislation, and a Bill for an Act may be brought forward as a result.

Parliament constitutes committees of its own members. These are either standing committees (that is, continuing ones) or committees set up for a particular purpose and therefore of limited duration.[2] Recommendations contained in such a committee's report to Parliament may lead to legislation. What are known as private or local Acts may originate in a request by a particular body for legislation to help it.

There is also the possibility of a private member of Parliament bringing forward a Bill which may ultimately be passed by Parliament as a statute. That possibility is a very limited one because, unless the government is prepared to support the Bill, it will receive a very low priority on Parliament's agenda ('the notice paper').

The minimal role of electors in the making of law by Parliament

Statutes seldom, if ever, owe their origin to a demand by the electors. Indeed, the electors as a group are a completely unorganised group. There is no machinery by which these electors can initiate legislation; and even public meetings called with a view to bringing pressure on the government for the passing of an Act will be attended by only a very small percentage of the total number of electors.

In a primitive society it is fair to assume that almost all, if not all, the members would know their society's laws. Today, however, the laws are so complex and so detailed that no elector who is not a practising lawyer would be likely to have any real conception of what Acts have in fact been passed. Indeed, even the lawyer has difficulty in keeping up with the reading of new Acts as

---

1   Churchill, Winston S (later Sir Winston Churchill), *The Second World War*, 1948, Cassel & Co Ltd, London, Vol V at 618.

2   See Parliamentary committees in Chapter 4.

they come out. The number of statutes made in each session of Parliament is considerable; the number that comes to the attention of the public is small.

In Switzerland and in California there is a legislative machinery by which a sufficient number of electors can originate the passing of an Act in the sense of demanding a referendum upon the topic. In Britain, there is no such provision. Indeed, particular pressure groups are more likely to prove effective than the electors as a whole because the pressure groups are organised, whereas the electors are not, and this is likely to be so even if (as is often the case) many of those in the pressure group are not electors in the relevant area.

The drafting of an Act of Parliament

The usual way in which an Act comes to be drafted is for instructions to be given by the minister concerned or by the Secretary of State or relevant department. It is then the task of the person who is to draft the proposed statute to be satisfied as to what is actually required and as to the extent to which that can be achieved within the powers of the Parliament and the policy of the government. This work involves an extensive knowledge of the Parliament's statutes, including the keeping of meticulous records of what amendments have been made and which of those amendments have actually come into force (many amendments are expressed to come into force when proclaimed).

The first step is to produce a draft Bill which is submitted to the Secretary of State or minister or to the departmental officers concerned (in the case of a Bill requested by a private member, the draft is of course submitted to that member). The first draft is not necessarily the Bill which is ultimately presented to Parliament. The Secretary of State, the minister or the departmental officers may have further ideas when they see the draft. There is nothing unusual about that: the difficulties inherent in drafting are such that anyone considering a draft legal document is likely to be able to see improvements. Again, that is not a criticism of the drafting: the very fact of having the draft in front of the person who sought it gives the opportunity of reconsidering the original ideas and thinking of additional ones. There may be several drafts of the Bill before it is finally brought before Parliament. The person who drafted the Bill attends in Parliament when the Bill is being debated, and is available to draft any amendments that may be required in the course of the debate.

The role of the governing parliamentary party

Parliament works on the party system except when the vote on a Bill is expressed to be a conscience vote. Each party has its own meeting room. In its meeting room the party in power in Parliament will consider legislation that it thinks should be brought forward, and it may consider legislation which the Cabinet has decided should be brought forward. The party in opposition will consider in its meeting room how best to mount an attack upon legislation before the House, or to criticise particular provisions of that legislation.

The meetings of the government party and of the opposition party in their consideration of legislation have a fundamentally different role to play. If the opposition party is not opposing the legislation as a whole, it is more likely to be concerned with matters of detail than is the government party. The party meeting of the party in power is more likely to be concerned with questions of principle than with questions of detail. Although the Cabinet is the executive body, it is obvious that the parliamentary party (that is, all the members of Parliament in the party in power) may give instructions to the Cabinet or the Secretary of State or minister in charge of the particular legislation or proposed legislation.

There are circumstances in which the party in power in Parliament would find it necessary or desirable to consider points of detail in the legislation. The need, or the desirability, could arise when the legislation is actually before the House. There may have been an attack by the Opposition on points of detail, and the governing party might well desire to consider the detail at this stage.

The importance of what is known as 'the party room' should not be underrated. In Parliament the Cabinet necessarily consists of only a small percentage of the members of Parliament in the governing party. Those members of Parliament who are not Secretaries of State or ministers (and those members of the opposition party who are not shadow ministers) are known as 'backbenchers'. There are occasions when the backbenchers of the governing party force their government to adopt, reject or modify legislation.

The role of the House of Lords

Not one of the members of the House of Lords has been elected to that House. Most, if not all, of those who are made life peers have been members of the House of Commons and can be expected to vote on party lines in favour of the party they have served in the Commons. Secretaries of State, ministers and shadow ministers are drawn from peers who are committed to one or other of the parties. With those exceptions, members of the House of Lords may consider each Bill on its merits irrespective of any party affiliations they may have. Consequently, and without any denigration of the Commons, the debate in the Lords is on a different level to the debate in the Lower House.

The role of the House of Lords has undergone a fundamental change since the early days of the evolution of Parliament. In those days it was for the monarch to decide whether those now known as the Commons would be invited to a sitting of Parliament. Indeed, 'In the first 25 years of Edward I's reign some 30 Parliaments were summoned, but there is evidence of the attendance of the Commons at only four'.[3] Today the function of the House of Lords is best described as that of a house of review. In that way valuable comments and criticisms may be made, but always bearing in mind that the House of Lords cannot reject a money Bill and that, if the Lords and the Commons disagree on a Bill and a reconciliation of the competing views is not achieved, the Bill may be reintroduced in the Commons. In those circumstances the second reading of the reintroduced Bill must be in one session and the third reading in another session one year later. The Bill can then become an Act without the consent of the House of Lords.

---

3   Mackenzie, KR, *The English Parliament*, 1950, Penguin Books Ltd, Harmondsworth at 17.

The role of Cabinet

The Cabinet may be regarded as the executive of the party which is in power in Parliament. Subject to any instructions it may be given from the party room, it is responsible for making decisions on policy. The actual implementation of that policy of course becomes the responsibility of individual Secretaries of State or ministers according to the fields of responsibility allotted to them.

Unless legislation has to be brought before Parliament with too much urgency for Cabinet as a whole to have the opportunity of considering it, draft legislation comes before the Cabinet prior to being introduced into Parliament. The extent to which it is considered by Cabinet, and the detail into which Cabinet will go in considering it, will depend upon the political importance of the particular legislation.

The parliamentary procedure for making an Act of Parliament

A Bill (which is the document which becomes the Act after it has been passed by Parliament) is 'read' a first time, a formal procedure authorising the Bill to be printed and distributed to all members of that House. It next receives its second reading. The second reading procedure commences with the Secretary of State or minister in charge of the Bill delivering a speech explaining what he or she understands the Bill to achieve (we use the term 'understands' because the wording and effect of the Bill may not in point of law achieve what the minister hopes the Bill will achieve). The Bill is then debated, the House resolving into committee to consider the various clauses of the Bill (these clauses are referred to as sections when the Bill becomes an Act). The Bill then receives its third reading. After the Bill has been passed by that House, it is sent to the other House of Parliament where it goes through the same procedure. If the other House decides to amend the Bill, it has to be sent back to the House in which it started for that House to consider the amendment. If the two Houses are in disagreement upon the amendment, each House appoints members who are called 'managers' and whose function it is to try to achieve agreement between the Houses. If agreement is not achieved, the Bill can be passed by the Commons alone (although with a year's delay) as mentioned in the preceding section of this chapter.

The timing of a Bill

The fact that a Bill has been read for the first time does not mean that it will immediately come before the House for a second reading. When it receives its second reading will depend upon the pressure of other measures before the House and upon the priority Cabinet decides to give it. It is possible for a Bill to be introduced into Parliament and its consideration by Parliament to be deferred to later in the same session or even until the next session of Parliament (a 'session' in this sense is not a particular day but extends over a period of weeks, or more usually months). This deferment is to enable Parliament to obtain the benefit of detailed criticism of the Bill by the public, or by the particular section of the public that would be affected by the legislation.

A private member's Bill will usually receive very low priority. As a result, it may not be able to be brought forward until after a lengthy waiting period. Indeed, unless the government of the day is prepared to adopt the private member's Bill, the private member may find it very difficult to obtain the passage of the legislation through Parliament at all.

Procedure after enactment

The fact that legislation has been enacted by Parliament does not of itself guarantee that it comes into force. It must first receive the royal assent.[4] Unless Parliament has expressly stated to the contrary in the particular Act, legislation comes into force on the day on which it receives the royal assent. However, Parliament with increasing frequency is providing for its legislation to come into force on some day subsequent to its receiving the royal assent. Parliament has even adopted the habit of providing for particular provisions of the Act to come into force on different days – a very confusing procedure, because it means that those affected by the Act have to check repeatedly as to whether or not particular provisions have come into force. The usual reason for deferring the coming into force of an Act, or of particular provisions of an Act, is the need to prepare subordinate legislation under the Act; but there may be other reasons in the particular case. For example, it may be thought desirable to defer the operation of an Act so as to enable those affected by it to make the necessary adjustments in their own business or other activities which will be controlled by the Act.

---

4   See The Crown in Chapter 4.

CHAPTER 6

INTERPRETING AN ACT OF PARLIAMENT

The need for statutes to be interpreted

An Act of Parliament cannot be applied automatically. It is a written document, and therefore to be applied it has to be interpreted: its meaning has to be ascertained by those who are to enforce it and by those who have to comply with it. Interpretation of an Act of Parliament is by no means easy. There may be, and often are, different ideas as to what the Act of Parliament means.

A need for interpretation may arise from:

(a) Imperfections in the use of language arising from failure to:

    (i) appreciate the meaning of the words used (eg 'charitable'); or

    (ii) realise that a particular word may have more than one meaning; or

    (iii) realise that the meaning of the word is changing (eg 'virtually').

(b) The fact that words do not have a single universally accepted meaning.

(c) Inadequacies in the instructions given to the drafter, resulting in a lack of awareness of existing circumstances within which the legislation must operate.

(d) Failure to foresee changed circumstances within which or new developments to which the legislation will have to be applied.

(e) Failure to revise the legislation when those circumstances change or those developments occur.

(f) Lack of technical knowledge on the part of the drafter when drafting legislation to operate in a technical field.

(g) Insufficient knowledge in the drafter of existing:

    (i) statutes and subordinate legislation; or

    (ii) judicial decisions; that insufficiency being contributed to by the lack of an effective index to statutes, subordinate legislation or common law.

(h) The haste with which the drafter is often expected to draft legislation.

(i) Several Acts dealing with the same subject matter in varying or inconsistent ways.

(j) Amendments that do not take sufficient cognisance of other provisions of the Act they are amending.

(k) A failure to use the same word in the same sense consistently throughout the Act.

(l) The overlooking of a statutory definition with consequent use of a word in other than the sense in which it is defined.

(m)Amendments that are made in a statute other than the statute being amended.

(n) The fact that most legislation is drafted in general terms but has to be applied to specific circumstances.

(o) Absurdity or injustice arising from the length of statutory provisions and the style of drafting.

The need for interpretation to resolve ambiguity in, or to overcome defective drafting of, an Act is increased by the fact that there is no separate skilled body to examine draft legislation prior to it being placed before Parliament.

Each of these causes of a need to interpret Acts of Parliament is considered in turn in the following pages.

Imperfections in the use of language

There is difficulty in ascertaining the intention of Parliament in some cases because language is imperfect. It may mean different things to different people, and words have a variety of meanings. The reference to orphans in the Gilbert and Sullivan opera *Pirates of Penzance* is frequently misunderstood because people fail to appreciate that an orphan is a person who has lost both parents *or either of them*.

There are words which have a special legal meaning which may be different from the meaning given to them in ordinary speech. For example, the word 'charitable' in ordinary speech is likely to mean benevolent, and, in particular, generous towards the poor (see the *Oxford English Dictionary*). In law, however, the word has a different meaning:

> That according to the law of England a technical meaning is attached to the word 'charity' and to the word 'charitable' in such expressions as 'charitable uses', 'charitable trusts' or 'charitable purposes', cannot, I think, be denied ... No doubt the popular meaning of the words 'charity' and 'charitable' does not coincide with their legal meaning ... but it is difficult to fix the point of divergence, and no one as yet has succeeded in defining the popular meaning of the word 'charity'.[1]

Thus in law 'activities which do not in any way affect the public or any section of it are not charitable',[2] yet for the lay person the giving of money to a family whose uninsured house was destroyed by fire would undoubtedly be regarded as charitable.

The word 'virtually' when used properly means 'in truth' (it comes from a Latin word meaning truth), but it is commonly used today in the sense of 'near enough'.

The fact that words do not have a single universally accepted meaning

People use words without realising that the meanings of those words are variable. A metre is a fixed standard of measurement. The term 'school', however, has a variety of meanings ranging from a comprehensive school to a public school, from a boys' school to a girls' school and a co-educational school, and from a music school to a tennis school and to a dancing school, and in

---

1   *Income Tax Special Purposes Commissioners v Pemsel* [1891] AC 531, Lord Macnaghten at 580–83.

2   *Re Warre's will trusts* [1953] 2 All ER 99, Harman J (later Harman LJ) at 101.

Vienna there is the world-famous Spanish Riding School. The view of a parent on the one hand and of a son or daughter on the other as to the meaning of 'child' may be quite different, particularly if the son or daughter wants to feel 'grown up'. The difference between a road and a street in law is that the street has houses along it whereas a road need not, but how many people use the two terms interchangeably?

When Parliament uses a word it will normally be thinking of the central or core meaning of that word. The members of Parliament have no time to think of every possible factual situation which may arise, and the drafter may be precluded from knowing of it because of the complexities of modern life; and it is therefore unlikely that the words which they have used will apply without difficulty to every possible factual situation. For example, everybody is likely to think they know what a 'building' is, yet do they? A house or shop or factory is a building. A caravan towed behind a car is not a building. But what of a caravan embedded in the ground with its wheels removed, electricity connected, and left there for six months? There are a large number of reported decisions of courts on the meaning of the word 'building', and the very nature of the word ensures that this must be so. So long as words cannot be made absolutely precise this problem will remain, and the need for interpretation will remain with it.

Inadequacies in the instructions given

The problems inherent in the present system of drafting legislation present the drafters with very real difficulties in ensuring that they produce draft legislation that accords with the intentions of those who are seeking the legislation. The department putting forward the legislation for drafting may not be fully aware of all the practical ramifications; and, indeed, it is unlikely to be so, for it lacks the practical experience. The instructions given to the drafter may be clear to the person giving them; but that clarity may depend upon the knowledge which is in the instructor's mind, and the instructor may therefore fail to convey what is necessary to the drafter. That is a very common defect of communication in the form of language. The drafter is also unlikely to have knowledge of the practical, and often technical, circumstances within which the legislation being drafted will be expected to operate: how is the drafter to have detailed knowledge of all the complex and highly technical aspects of our involved modern society?

Failure to foresee changed circumstances

There is legislation drafted before the advent of motorcars, before radio transmission, before television. How could the drafter of those days foresee how the circumstances to which it is to be applied would change? Even the drafter working with all due care in the late 1940s would be unlikely to have foreseen the Internet.

Failure to revise the legislation

Parliament may have used words which were quite appropriate to the state of scientific knowledge at the time, but which cause difficulties once scientific knowledge has been extended.

Lack of technical knowledge

Life is becoming increasingly specialised, and what may appear perfectly sensible to a person inexperienced in a particular field may cause problems which could only be foreseen by an expert. In such a case, the difficulty is not likely to be discovered by either the drafter or the members of Parliament, but only when the attempt is made to apply the new law.

Insufficient knowledge

There is a maze of statutes, subordinate legislation and judicial decisions. Specialist drafters of course build up an extensive library and extensive records to enable them to find the relevant statutory provisions or other aspects of the law. Nevertheless, they have very real difficulties in carrying out their searches. As any lawyer knows, it is very easy to miss a statutory provision, even easier to miss subordinate legislation, and often difficult to find particular aspects of legal decisions contained in the various law reports.

Drafting in urgency

Drafting a document with clarity is a surprisingly difficult task. Lawyers skilled in this sphere have found that there is a great advantage to putting the document aside once they have drafted it, and leaving it for consideration perhaps a fortnight or a month later. That cooling-off period enables the drafter to examine the document critically: examining it immediately after drafting it does not have the same advantage because the drafter is too fresh in the task. The drafter who attempts to examine critically what has been drafted as soon as it has been drafted knows what it was intended to say and will be too likely to assume that that has in fact been achieved. Unfortunately, those drafting Bills for Parliament to consider usually lack the advantage of being able to set the document aside for a cooling-off period. In so many instances their work is required in a hurry. Repeatedly, the drafter must produce legislation for introduction into Parliament even on the same day. Of course, not all legislation is drafted with that degree of urgency; and many important Bills are the subject of a number of drafts before they finally reach Parliament. Nevertheless, urgency is a real problem in this field.

Several Acts dealing with the same subject matter

Parliament does not always deal with each topic of legislation in a single Act. Many Acts cover several topics of legislation, and conversely many topics of legislation are covered by several Acts.

Failure to consider other provisions of the same Act

Many Acts of Parliament have been amended very frequently. Just to ensure that each Act is fully up to date is not easy, even for members of the legal profession. This is particularly the case with regard to Community legislation, notwithstanding the convention of referring in the preamble in the text to the last amending instrument. These amendments are made at different times, often over a period of years, and it is inevitable that sooner or later amendments will fail to fit properly into the patchwork.

Failure to use the same word in the same sense throughout

Partly because of the length of many statutes, and partly because of the number of times that statutes are amended (often by persons other than those who drafted the original Act), it is difficult to use the same word in the same sense throughout the Act and its amendments. Obviously, if the meaning of the word changes through the Act, difficulties do arise in interpreting the Act.

Overlooking a statutory definition

Acts of Parliament often contain a large number of definitions. These are to be found not only in the definitions section near the end of the Act, but in other places as well. The Housing Act 1985 had 625 sections. It is only by starting at the end of the Act and working backwards to section 622 that the reader finds 22 definitions set out in alphabetical order, yet even that section is not comprehensive: six definitions are contained in section 621, a further two in section 623, and at least another 224 are to be found scattered through numerous sections. Some of the definitions apply to a specified subsection, others to a section, others to a part of the Act, and others to the whole Act. Even that maze does not suffice, for the reader finds that the Act, in addition to its 625 sections, has 24 schedules, and in those schedules there are a further 53 definitions. To add to the complexity, various of the definitions do not actually state the meaning but by incorporating a definition that appears in another statute they send the reader chasing after that Act also.

The reader whose paperchase had revealed the 287 definitions of the Housing Act might assume that the chase was complete, but no: for over a century there has been legislation specifying definitions that are applicable to all statutes unless expressly excluded.[3] Those definitions, too, have therefore to be researched and applied.

Amendments that are made in a statute other than the statute being amended

An unfortunate aspect of the drafting of Bills is that amendments do not have to appear in the statute they are amending. This lack of such a requirement results

---

3   See the Interpretation Act 1889 and its successor the Interpretation Act 1978.

in amendments being inserted in statutes of totally different names to the statute being amended. Where should the reader turn to find an amendment (a partial repeal) of the Consumer Credit Act 1974? That amendment is effected by Schedule 6 Clean Air Act 1993. An amendment of the National Heritage Act 1983 is made in Schedule 21 Leasehold Reform, Housing and Urban Development Act 1993. An amendment of s 9 Agricultural Holdings Act 1948 is to be found in s 23(1) Housing Act 1985. Beware!

Legislation in general terms has to be applied to specific circumstances

The drafter of a Bill may find it appropriate to be specific in formulating its requirements. For example, legislation which empowers an authorised person to remove a vehicle from a street requires that: 'Before a vehicle ... is entered, opened or removed ... the local authority shall notify the police of the intention to take action ...'.[4] That requirement is specific. It is more likely, however, that a statute will be expressed in general terms which will have to be applied to a specific need probably long after that statute came into force. The question then arises as to how the terms of the statute are to be interpreted and whether they are capable of meeting the changed circumstances. It is very unlikely that even in the 1940s the drafter of legislation on nuisances would have envisaged the changes brought about by the community views on the environment that became of such importance only two decades later. Would the drafter foresee, for example, the asbestos nuisance which has caused such concern in the insurance world? Would such a drafter foresee that before the end of the 20th century environmental legislation would have grown to a statute with 712 subsections spread through 125 sections and 24 schedules comprising a total of 488 clauses?[5]

Absurdity or injustice

Although of course the drafter endeavours to draft legislation in such a way that there is neither absurdity nor injustice in its provisions, the courts have repeatedly drawn attention to the fact that absurdity or injustice has occurred. For example, in the Court of Appeal, Lord Denning MR refused to apply the literal meaning of words because he said that literal meaning:

> Gives rise to such an absurd result that there must be some mistake in drafting. Such mistakes do occur from time to time: and when they occur, the courts must do what they can to put things right. I think that the courts should correct these words.[6]

---

4   Schedule 3, para 2A Environmental Protection Act 1990 as inserted by s 4 Noise and
    Statutory Nuisance Act 1993.

5   Environment Act 1995.

6   *Camden London Borough Council v Post Office* [1977] 1 WLR 892 at 897.

The role of statutory interpretation

Although those whose duty it is to enforce an Act of Parliament must necessarily interpret that Act, and although those who are bound by the Act must necessarily interpret it also, their views upon its meaning may differ – and they frequently do. Indeed, the meaning of statutes is a constant source of litigation. There must necessarily be an arbiter to decide between the conflicting views. That is the role of the judge. The judge is the one who must decide what the Act means. In so deciding, the judge is not bound to agree with one side or the other: the judge must decide what is the right interpretation to place upon the legislation even if neither of the opposing parties has contended for that particular meaning – 'it is an exercise of the judicial power of the state, and consequently a function of the judiciary alone, to interpret the written law when made'.[7]

Does the judge, in carrying out the judicial function of interpreting an Act of Parliament, merely interpret, or does the judge actually make law? It has been held repeatedly by the courts that, if Parliament fails to cover a particular aspect of the matter to which the statute relates, it is for Parliament and not for the courts to fill the gap. Such a gap is known to lawyers as a *casus omissus*. In such a case the Act must be read as it stands, and must therefore be read as failing to deal with that matter.[8]

It is the role of the court to interpret the statute according to the intention of Parliament insofar as that intention can be discovered from the words that Parliament has used in the statute itself. As Lord Radcliffe has expressed it, 'every statute is to be expounded according to its manifest and express intention'.[9] Of course, opinions as to what the intention of Parliament really was may differ. The ordinary reader may well think that, in ascertaining the intention of Parliament and interpreting the Act according to that inferred intention, the court is legislating instead of interpreting. For example, although an Act constituting a board stated that 'every decision or determination of a board shall be final', the Court of Appeal held that it had power to declare that the board's decision was wrong. Denning LJ (later Lord Denning MR) said:

> The remedy is not excluded by the fact that the determination of the board is by statute made 'final'. Parliament only gives the impress of finality to the decisions of the board on the condition that they are reached in accordance with the law, and the Queen's courts can issue a declaration to see that this condition is fulfilled.[10]

The reality is that there are certain basic principles and rights, and the courts will be reluctant to believe that Parliament intended to interfere with matters of such basic importance.

---

7   *Chokolingo v Attorney General* [1981] 1 WLR 106 at 110–11.

8   See, for example, *Mersey Docks & Harbour Board v Henderson* (1888) 13 App Cas 595, Lord Halsbury at 603.

9   *Attorney General (Canada) v Hallett & Carey Ltd* [1952] AC 427 at 449.

10   *Taylor v National Assistance Board* [1957] P 101 at 111; affirmed, [1958] AC 532.

The rules of statutory interpretation

It is important that statutes be interpreted consistently. If each judge were free to interpret Acts in his or her own way, confusion would arise. To achieve that consistency the courts have developed a series of rules to be applied in interpreting Acts. The need for those rules is apparent. Anyone who is familiar with the difficulties of statutory interpretation would wholeheartedly agree with Lord Loreburn who, as Lord Chancellor of England, said in the course of a judicial decision:

> From early times courts of law have been continuously obliged, in endeavouring loyally to carry out the intentions of Parliament, to observe a series of familiar precautions for interpreting statutes so imperfect and obscure as they often are.[11]

The 'familiar precautions' to which Lord Loreburn there referred are what are known as the rules of statutory interpretation. It is important that the person trying to understand an Act of Parliament is aware of those rules and knows how to use them. An Act of Parliament cannot be read as a novel. It must be read according to the established rules. Those rules are set out and explained with examples in *How to Understand an Act of Parliament*.[12]

One of the rules used by the courts in interpreting an Act is that the Act is to be interpreted according to the intention of Parliament. However, the rule requires that intention to be ascertained from the Act itself. The court cannot ask the minister, or the Cabinet, or even Parliament itself what was meant by the Act. Departmental circulars and ministerial statements about the Act cannot be used in interpreting it (this is a very important and very sound rule, for departmental circulars or ministerial statements based upon what the department or the minister intended may be very different to what Parliament in fact passed).

Another rule is that the courts in interpreting the Act are limited to what appears in the Act as passed by Parliament. They must follow what Parliament has actually said, not what a reform group might have liked it to say. This is so even if the Act originated in pressure from that reform group. Reformers may feel themselves frustrated by this principle of statutory interpretation, but it is basic to the rule of law. If this principle were not applied, it would be interpretation by the reformers and not by the courts; and it would be the words of the reformers expressed after the Act had been passed and the dispute had arisen, and not the words of Parliament itself which would prevail.

Originally the common law allowed *Hansard* to be used only to discover the mischief the Act is intended to cure and precluded the use of *Hansard* to find out directly the meaning of the Act.[13] The House of Lords, however, has changed the common law, and *Hansard* can now be used to find the meaning of the Act.[14]

---

11 *Nairn v University of St Andrews* [1909] AC 147 at 161.

12 By Gifford, DJ (PhD Cantab) and Salter, John R (MA Oxon), 1996, London, Cavendish Publishing Limited, the first of the *How to Understand* series.

13 *Millar v Taylor* (1769) 4 Burr 2303 at 2332.

14 *Pepper v Hart* [1993] AC 593, Lord Browne-Wilkinson at 634.

There are in fact numerous rules that have to be applied in deciding what meaning is to be placed upon a provision in a statute. There is the rule that the marginal notes are not to be used in finding the meaning of the Act, and there is the rule that headings to parts and divisions of the Act are to be used if necessary. There is the rule that the setting out of some things expressly in the Act impliedly excludes all others, and there are many other rules. Reference in this regard should be made to *How to Understand an Act of Parliament*,[15] each of the rules being dealt with in turn in that book.

---

15 By Gifford, DJ (PhD Cantab) and Salter, John R (MA Oxon), 1996, London, Cavendish Publishing Limited, the first of the *How to Understand* series.

CHAPTER 7

SUBORDINATE LEGISLATION

The nature of subordinate legislation

The nature and forms of subordinate legislation have already been considered in Chapter 2. Subordinate legislation is often referred to as delegated legislation. The two terms are interchangeable.

The way in which power is delegated

Parliament confers power to make delegated or subordinate legislation by setting out that power in a statute. It may do so in specific terms, or it may confer a broader, more general, power.

The authorities to which power is commonly delegated

In order to understand how subordinate legislation is made, it is necessary to draw a distinction between the person who prepared the subordinate legislation and the person who actually makes it. Thus there are numerous provisions in Acts of Parliament empowering the making of subordinate legislation by the Secretary of State or minister charged with the administering of an Act. In such a case the initiative for the subordinate legislation may in fact come from the minister. Obviously, it could also come from the Cabinet or from the party room. The fact that the initiative can come from those quarters does not, however, preclude the department or statutory authority concerned from bringing proposed subordinate legislation before the Secretary of State or minister; and in practice by far the majority of subordinate legislation made by a Secretary of State or minister owes its origin to the government department or statutory authority under his or her administration. The power to make subordinate legislation is conferred by Parliament upon statutory authorities.

The reasons for delegation

There is a variety of reasons why Parliament may choose to delegate the power to legislate. In practice, however, such delegation has become so well established within the government framework of our communities that it is difficult to point to any one reason as being the cause of delegation in any particular case. One of the major causes of the conferring of power to make subordinate legislation, and perhaps indeed the major cause, is to be found in the growing complexity of modern society and the growth of bureaucracy that has gone with it.

Another major cause is the drain upon parliamentary time. Whether Parliament should sit on more days (or nights) of the year than it in fact does, is a topic that excites the interest of the media from time to time. However strong the arguments that may be put for or against the average number of sitting days for Parliament, it has to be borne in mind that Secretaries of State, ministers and committee chairmen have many duties outside Parliament itself and that, unless they have sufficient time for those duties, a fundamental basis of the parliamentary system would cease to exist: it is fundamental for our parliamentary system that there is the doctrine of ministerial responsibility whereby a Secretary of State or minister is responsible to Parliament and has to answer to Parliament for the actions of his or her department and of any statutory authority within his or her portfolio. It is also fair to bear in mind that members of Parliament (whether Secretaries of State, ministers, shadow ministers, or backbenchers) have many duties to their electorates which must necessarily be performed outside Parliament.

Two other reasons for subordinate legislation need to be noted. One is that Parliament, when enacting legislation, may have approved the concept of control of the relevant subject matter without having before it any of the material necessary to a detailed working out of the control. The other is that departments find it advantageous to legislate under delegated authority rather than to depend upon the obtaining of specific legislation.

Advantages of delegation

The desirability of subordinate legislation is something on which opinions differ. It has, as so often in life, advantages and disadvantages. Whatever the relative merits, and whatever the relative weight, of those advantages and disadvantages, the fact is that subordinate legislation is with us, and is apparently with us to stay. One great advantage of subordinate legislation is that it gives greater flexibility. Despite the fact that there are numerous amending Acts, it is much easier to amend a statutory instrument such as a regulation, rule or order than a statute. The formalities required to amend subordinate legislation are much less than those required to amend an Act.

Incorporating in an Act of Parliament a provision for subordinate legislation is regarded as saving parliamentary, and thereby ministerial, time. When the device of delegating the power to legislate is used extensively in an Act, or major matters which would otherwise have to be included in the Act are left to the person or body upon whom the power is conferred, the Act itself is shortened. In some cases Parliament does no more than approve the concept of control of the particular subject matter and leaves the whole of the working out of the control to a statutory body or to a department. Such an approach leaves less to engage the attention of the Opposition and therefore enables legislation to be enacted more speedily. Another advantage of subordinate legislation is that it places the authority to legislate in the hands of those expert in the particular field.

Disadvantages of delegation

One of the most important disadvantages of the extensive use of subordinate legislation provisions is that they amount to an abdication of its role by Parliament. If it be accepted that the function of Parliament is to legislate, how can it be said to be discharging that function when it leaves vital provisions (and in some cases most of the vital provisions) to be formulated by persons who have no responsibility to the electorate at all? Such a delegation carries with it the disadvantage of increasing the power of the administrator with the correlative disadvantages of rubber-stamping of bureaucratic decisions and of lack of effective control.

The difficulty of finding subordinate legislation is referred to in Chapter 3. It is a very real disadvantage of subordinate legislation, as all who have to find out what particular controls are in existence know only too well.

Court supervision of subordinate legislation

There is a limited extent to which subordinate legislation is subject to supervision by the courts. It must not be imagined that the judges, or any one or more of the judges, have the responsibility of examining subordinate legislation as it is made. The only way in which the supervisory function of the courts comes into play is if some person challenges the legality of a particular statutory instrument. It should be noted, too, that a challenge may be more limited than that, extending only to part of the statutory instrument. Upon such a challenge it is not the responsibility of the court to consider the desirability or otherwise of a particular piece of subordinate legislation that is under attack, and it does not even have the power to do so. All that the court can do is to consider whether or not subordinate legislation complies with the legal requirements applicable to it. Moreover, in what is undoubtedly the leading case, it has been held that statutory instruments made by public representative bodies such as councils:

> ... ought to be supported if possible. They ought to be, as has been said, 'benevolently' interpreted, and credit ought to be given to those who have to administer them that they will be reasonably administered.[1]

In addition, the courts have adopted the view that the electors have adequate control over the councillors of their local authority. The approach so adopted by the courts can be well illustrated by what was said by Lawton LJ in the English Court of Appeal:

> In my judgment this court should be most reluctant to interfere with the exercise of ... powers by a local authority. Local authorities have to meet the electors from time to time. The electors are in a far better position than this court ever could be to decide whether the powers have been exercised in a way which meets with general approval.[2]

When, however, what is at issue is whether the statutory instrument is within the powers delegated by Parliament, it is not 'general approval' but the court's interpretation of the Act and of the statutory instrument that must prevail.

---

1 *Kruse v Johnson* [1892] 2 QB 91 at 99.
2 *Bristol District Council v Clark* [1975] 1 WLR 1443 at 1449.

CHAPTER 8

HOW JUDGES DEVELOP THE LAW

The hierarchy of the courts

Reference has been made[1] to the fact that there is a hierarchy of courts. Indeed, in any developed system of law such a hierarchy is inevitable. The different levels of tribunals and courts are differently constituted, and handle different kinds of problems. The lower levels of the hierarchy, such as magistrates' courts, handle problems in which the issues of fact are usually more to the forefront in the litigation than are issues of law. Also, the amounts of money at stake are usually less than in litigation before the higher levels of the hierarchy. What is needed is a practical common sense approach – provided that Parliament only entrusts cases of such a nature to this level of the hierarchy. Unfortunately, Parliament does not always observe the distinction.

Development of the law by tribunals and by courts of less than superior court status

Tribunals, and courts of less than superior court status, give decisions which are important to the parties appearing before them. Their decisions do not form part of the common law. However, in the case of specialised courts and tribunals their decisions do form a body of principles which are of importance in their particular specialised fields.

The consumption of alcohol has been a problem in the community probably for as long as alcohol has existed. There are, unfortunately, those who cannot hold their liquor. The attempt by the United States of America to introduce a prohibition upon the sale of alcohol failed dismally, in fact leading to highly organised crime and to open warfare between competing gangs in the prohibition era. The Islamic world prohibits the consumption of alcohol, and enforces its prohibition by rigorous penalties – penalties that become notorious from time to time when public floggings of offenders hit the headlines in the media. The approach which has been universally adopted in the western world today is not that of prohibition but that of control. To achieve that control Parliament has enacted legislation to regulate and control the liquor industry. That legislation renders the making, limiting and refusing of licences a matter of judicial decision. The judicial decisions are by justices and are therefore not part of the common law, but they naturally become known to those whose livelihood is in the liquor industry, and they of course become known also to the lawyers specialising in this field of law. Whilst not part of the common law, they do therefore serve a valuable purpose by developing a coherent body of principles known to those appearing before the court and known to those who have to conform to its requirements.

---

1   See Common law in Chapter 2.

Town planning is another very important field. The amounts at stake in a planning appeal may be far beyond those ordinarily involved in superior court litigation, but Parliament has entrusted the hearing of planning appeals to departmental inspectors. Very occasionally a planning appeal has been heard by a Queen's Counsel. The Secretary of State has power to decide an appeal and has exercised that power in a significant number of appeals, but of the 25,000 planning appeals heard each year the overwhelming number are decided by the inspector. Decisions by inspectors establish town planning principles which are of value to planning authorities, town planning consultants, applicants for permits, and objectors to applications for permits, and which must certainly be studied and known by lawyers specialising in this very extensive field. These bodies are dealing with matters which are of great importance either to an individual (as, for instance, whether that individual is to have the right to construct a home on his or her own land) or to the community (as, for instance, in the establishment of large new industries).

Development of the law by courts of superior court status

There was a time when judges and lawyers claimed that the courts did not make law but simply set out the principles of the common law that had always been there. Even today, there are judges who are reluctant to be seen to be making law. Nevertheless, in a time of rapid social change, the need for change in the law is so great that the courts have been forced to develop the common law principles to meet the new social needs. Today it is recognised that judges of the superior courts do make law, although they are expected to do so by developing existing principles rather than by striking out on their own. Judges who gain a reputation for attempting to force the pace of development of the law, even judges of the status of Lord Denning MR, are likely to be brought sharply to heel by the highest courts in the hierarchy.

It must be remembered that the main aim of a court, of whatever status, is not to develop the law in general but to find a just solution to a dispute between the parties in a particular case. The development of the law therefore depends upon a suitable fact situation coming before a court of sufficient status.

The doctrine of precedent

The nature of the doctrine of precedent has already been considered in Chapter 2.[2]

The basis of the doctrine of precedent

The doctrine of precedent is based on the view that what has been decided by the superior courts should remain valid and be accepted as law until it has either been overruled by a higher court in the same hierarchy, or altered by Act of Parliament. Even if a decision may be criticised by academics of standing and by practising lawyers, it may be better to have certainty in the law rather than a

---

2   See Common law in Chapter 2.

welter of conflicting decisions or even frequent change. There are many instances, particularly in the life of the commercial community, in which it is preferable for the parties to a dispute to know what their legal position is rather than to engage in the pursuit of perfecting the law.

The doctrine of precedent is applied strictly to all levels in the hierarchy except the very highest. For example, all courts below the House of Lords are bound by House of Lords' decisions but the House of Lords is able to overrule its own earlier decisions, although it is naturally reluctant to do so.

The extent to which a decision constitutes a precedent

Decisions as precedents may be either binding or persuasive. Whether they are binding on the one hand or persuasive on the other depends upon the hierarchy of the courts. If the precedent is a decision given by a court to which there is a right of appeal from the court in which the precedent is cited, the decision is a binding precedent. Thus, a decision of the Court of Appeal is a binding precedent so far as the courts of the High Court of Justice are concerned. All other precedents are said to be persuasive: a decision of the Court of Session is a persuasive, not a binding, precedent in England.

Whether a court is bound by its own previous decisions

The Judicial Committee of the Privy Council has never held itself to be bound by its own previous decisions, although it will of course ordinarily follow them. The House of Lords regarded itself as bound by its own decisions until 1964. It now holds itself free to overrule its previous decisions, but only in exceptional cases. Even although a court is not bound by its own prior decisions it will ordinarily follow them because of the consequent advantage of certainty in the law.

How a court uses a precedent

In real life, fact situations are rarely exactly the same. In successive legal actions the details of the facts, even in cases which are in some respects quite similar, are likely to differ. Under the doctrine of precedent the courts are concerned with the principles of earlier decisions rather than with every detail of the fact situations in the earlier cases. This gives a court the opportunity either to extend or to limit an earlier principle.

In *Donoghue v Stevenson*[3] a man purchased a bottle of soft drink over the counter and gave some to his girlfriend. After she had drunk some, she claimed to have found the rotten remains of a snail in the soft drink bottle. She claimed that, as a result of drinking the soft drink with the decomposed snail in it, she became ill; and she sued the manufacturer of the soft drink for damages. The House of Lords laid down the principle that the manufacturer should have been able to foresee that negligence in the manufacture of the soft drink might cause

---

3   [1932] AC 562.

harm to anyone who drank that soft drink. The test adopted by the House of Lords at that time was a test of 'who is my neighbour?'. The principle established by the House of Lords in *Donoghue v Stevenson* was not, of course, confined to manufacturers of soft drink, and it was not confined to decomposed snails in soft drink.

The principle was applied in a case in which the negligence by the manufacturer did not relate to soft drink, or to drink, or even to food at all. The manufacturer was a manufacturer of underwear. The manufacturer used certain substances in the cleansing of the wool as a step in the manufacture of the underwear, and negligently failed to remove all of those substances in the course of manufacture. As a result, a purchaser of the underwear developed a skin complaint. The manufacturer was held liable in damages to the purchaser of the underwear, the Privy Council applying the principle in *Donoghue v Stevenson*.[4]

If a precedent is binding upon a court, that court is of course obliged to follow that binding precedent. If it fails to do so, its decision can be set aside by appealing to the appropriate court above it in the hierarchy of courts. Even if a precedent is one which binds the particular court, it is not everything that is contained in the reasons for decision in the precedent that must be followed by that court. Sometimes a judge expresses views in the course of the decision which are not essential to the decision of the case. Those views are known to lawyers as *obiter dicta* and are not binding upon courts deciding subsequent cases – although, of course, the judge deciding a subsequent case may find the obiter dicta set out a useful course to follow.

The decisions of courts in a different hierarchy are not binding precedents because there is no right of appeal from the particular court to the court in that other hierarchy which decided the case. Similarly, the decision of a judge of the same court as the judge deciding the new case is not binding because there is no right of appeal from the one judge to the other. However, the decision of a judge of the same court would be likely to persuade the judge in the later case to apply the same principles. Also, if the Scottish Court of Session establishes a principle in one of its decisions and a comparable situation arises in an English court the English judge may find the decision of the Court of Session a useful precedent to follow. Precedents of this nature are described as 'persuasive' precedents.

Lawyers use various technical terms to describe the way in which a court, whether lower or higher in the hierarchy than the court which decided the earlier case, treats that earlier decision. If a decision of a lower court is taken on appeal to a higher court in the same hierarchy its decision may be *reversed*. This means that the decision of the lower court is no longer of any effect, even between the same parties. The decision of the court on appeal replaces the earlier decision for all purposes. Alternatively, the higher court may uphold the earlier decision, in which case the earlier decision is said to be *affirmed* on appeal.

---

4   *Grant v Australian Knitting Mills Ltd* [1936] AC 85.

Not all cases are taken on appeal, even when there are grounds for thinking that the decision of the lower court may be wrong. For example, the party who lost before the lower court may not have sufficient funds or the matter may not be of sufficient importance to risk an appeal. Alternatively, the matter may be too urgent to allow time for an appeal. In such a case, when the earlier decision comes up for consideration again before a higher court in the same hierarchy in a later case, the original parties to the earlier decision will not be represented before the higher court, and its decision will not affect the results of the earlier decision as it applies to them. If the higher court decides that the earlier decision was wrong it will *overrule* that decision. If it decides that the earlier decision was right, the higher court will *approve* it. A decision which is overruled is no longer a precedent for the future (although its past effects, as between the original parties, remain). If it is approved, it gains added weight and authority because it now has the support of a higher court in the same hierarchy.

Where a court has to consider the decision of a court in another hierarchy, it may still *approve* of that decision, but it cannot *reverse* that decision because there is no appeal from one court to the other. In such a case, if the later court thinks the earlier decision was wrong, it will *disapprove* of it. The decision disapproved of still remains a valid precedent in the hierarchy in which it was decided, but its authority in the hierarchy a court of which disapproved of it is very much weakened (or, depending on the status of the court disapproving of it, destroyed); and the fact that it has been disapproved of is likely to be taken into account by courts in that other hierarchy when next the particular principle arises for consideration by them.

When a court does not wish to destroy the authority of an earlier decision in the circumstances in which that earlier decision was made, or when it lacks the authority to do so, and yet does not wish to apply the principles set out in the earlier case to the case presently before it, it may *distinguish* the earlier decision. In doing so, the later court sets out some reason, or reasons, why the principles laid down in the earlier decision do not apply in the present circumstances.

Precedent as restricting the development of the legal system

The doctrine of precedent, by its very nature, is resistant to drastic or sudden change. Once a principle has been laid down by a court of high status in the hierarchy, it is very difficult to remove or substantially alter that principle. The difficulty of removing or altering such a principle increases with the length of time that has passed since that principle was laid down. During that time, however, social conditions may have changed, and a doctrine or principle which was once appropriate may have become very inappropriate in the social conditions now prevailing. For example, the courts had developed a doctrine of 'common employment'. This doctrine stated that when an injury to one servant was caused by another servant of the same master, the master would not be liable in damages to the injured servant, although the other servant would be.[5]

---

5   *Priestly v Fowler* (1837) 3 M&W 1.

This doctrine was a sensible one in the conditions of domestic employment 100 years ago, when the number of servants would be few and when each servant would have a personal relationship with the others. The doctrine is wholly inappropriate to modern factory employment, when the 'servants' may number thousands and may not know each other personally at all. Because of the doctrine of precedent the principle of 'common employment' lingered on long after its usefulness was spent. The courts managed to modify it by holding it to be inapplicable if there was a breach of statutory duty by the employer.[6]

In the case of an inappropriate principle of law laid down many years ago by the highest court in a hierarchy, only that court (or, of course, Parliament) has the power to get rid of it. In the case of a principle laid down by a court of lower status, the principle will remain until some litigant takes the considerable risk of challenging the established state of the law in a legal action: no matter how strongly an individual judge, or judges generally, may hold the view that the principle established by the earlier case should be changed, there is no power in them to make that change until litigation arises which raises the particular issue.

Precedent as developing the law

The doctrine of precedent provides a means by which the law can be developed. Although the doctrine makes it difficult to get rid of inappropriate principles, it enables appropriate principles to be established on a firm basis. The abandonment of the doctrine of precedent would produce a welter of conflicting decisions, all judges deciding as seemed best to them, with little regard for decisions in previous cases on similar facts. This can be seen in the case of administrative tribunals which sit in divisions, where one division adopts a principle which conflicts with principles adopted by another division of the same tribunal. In such circumstances, the success or failure of a litigant will depend not so much upon the facts of the case as upon the division of the tribunal which hears it. The European Court has no doctrine of precedent.

The doctrine of precedent encourages the development of the law in a consistent and coherent fashion. Principles of law are developed gradually, and the courts in later cases have the opportunity either to expand or to restrict the area within which a particular principle will be applied. It is likely that a number of cases will have been heard by the lower courts before the highest court in the hierarchy is required to consider a new principle: in such a case the highest court will have the benefit of the opinions of various other judges, and can see how the new principle is behaving in a variety of fact situations. The doctrine of precedent therefore encourages the development of principles which are appropriate in the fact situations and social circumstances of the time of its establishment. The doctrine of precedent means that old cases still retain some authority. A principle which centuries ago had only a small area of applicability may, in modern social conditions, find fertile soil for growth. For example, the doctrine of 'abuse of public office', under which a public official may be held

---

6   *Groves v Wimborne* [1898] 2 QB 402.

liable in damages to the citizen for abuse of power, lay dormant for 100 years until the vast growth of bureaucracy made it important to have such a doctrine to protect the citizen's rights. The doctrine was revived in England in 1957 by the Court of Appeal.[7]

Some major areas of development of the law through precedent

Having regard to the way in which precedents are established it is not surprising to find that the development of the law in particular fields occurs as those fields become of importance within the community. Indeed, in this regard, the series of law reports become a social history. In England during the 19th century the great matter of public concern was railways. As early as 1839 the courts had to decide the then important question as to what constitutes a railway station[8] (the very reference to the series of law reports shows the importance of railways at that time in the social history of England, for it was a set of law reports confined to railway and canal cases). By 1885 even the House of Lords had been called upon to decide what constitutes a 'passenger train'.[9]

Today the growth areas of precedent are the fields of liability, administrative law, and the law relating to the environment. These are the matters of concern in the modern community, that concern is reflected in the growth of litigation in these fields, and consequently precedents arise and principles are developed to meet the changing situation. Decisions which would not have been dreamt of by lawyers 30 years ago are commonplace today.

---

7 *Wood v Blair & Helmsley Rural District Council* (1957) 4 ALR 243.

8 *Eton College (Provost) v Great Western Railway Co* (1839) 1 Ry and Can Cas 200.

9 *Burnett v Great North of Scotland Railway Co* (1885) 10 App Cas 147.

CHAPTER 9

HOW EFFECTIVE IS OUR LAW-MAKING PROCESS?

Parliament

Before the growth of the present party system, Parliament was a debating house. Representatives of the wealthier citizens were elected as members of Parliament to bring the people's grievances before the government and if possible to achieve redress. As the power of Parliament grew, it became the custom to form the government out of those people who could maintain a leading position in Parliament itself. At that time personalities were very important, and each political figure would have those who followed him, those who opposed him, and many who were neutral. The art of forming a government at that time was that of choosing as ministers those who could bring the maximum parliamentary support to the new government. While parties did exist, they did not have the rigid organisation of the modern political party; and it was not essential for a member of Parliament to be in, and remain in, the one political party. Because the government and the leaders of the parties could not always rely on the unthinking support of those who were counted as members of those parties, it was important not merely to put forward legislation as party legislation, but actually to justify it in a debate in Parliament itself. The increasing rigidity of the modern party system means that any real debate (except on the rare private member's bill) is almost impossible. How rare it is can be seen from the fact that it is sometimes necessary to have a 'free conscience vote' in which each member of Parliament can vote as he or she wishes, regardless of party. The rarity of such votes shows just how rigid the party system has become. Indeed, even at a time when the party system in Parliament was less rigid than it is today, WS Gilbert satirised the position in *Iolanthe*:

> When in that House MPs divide,
> If they've a brain and cerebellum, too,
> They've got to leave that brain outside,
> And vote just as their leaders tell 'em to.
> But then the prospect of a lot of dull MPs in close proximity,
> All thinking for themselves, is what
> No man can face with equanimity.

The rigidity of the party system results in very few amendments put forward by the Opposition in the House of Commons being accepted. The House of Lords, with its membership on a different basis to that of the Commons, debates in a different atmosphere and therefore has a greater opportunity of putting forward amendments that may prove acceptable to the government.

At one time Parliament at least had control of all major national legislation. There were, of course, local byelaws and the rules governing members of guilds, but new law affecting the nation as a whole was made either by Parliament or by the courts. Nowadays, a great bulk of new law is provided by subordinate legislation. The vast increase in the bulk of this type of legislation, and the very limited control which Parliament now has over it, limit the effectiveness of Parliament itself. The average member of Parliament, like the ordinary citizen, would be unaware of the contents of most of this subordinate legislation.

Courts

The courts of common law have centuries of experience behind them in making and applying the law. The common law is still perfectly capable of developing new fields of law as the need arises. However, its effectiveness is limited by the growing number of decisions, which in turn results from increasing population and increasing litigation. Particularly in the United States of America, with its huge number of State Supreme Courts as well as the Federal Courts hierarchy, it has become impossible even for the judges to keep up with the flood of new decisions throughout the country. The use of computers will help the lawyer to know which decisions may be relevant, but it still takes time to read them. Moreover, the flood of new law (both common law and statutory) makes it increasingly difficult for the lawyer to keep abreast of new law as it appears.

The 20th century has been a time of rapid economic development and social change. The law, while in many fields it has developed very considerably, has not kept place with this change in other fields. Although 'one of the great merits of the common law is that it is usually sufficiently flexible to take account of the changing needs of the continually changing society'[1] the judges, in most cases, dislike making new departures in the law; and the more fundamental the departure which they are asked to make, the less likely they are to make it.

The very fact that Parliament has taken such a large role this century in the development of the law has resulted in the more conservative judges using Parliament as a crutch. Faced with Parliament's obvious concern that the law should be developed to meet changing social needs, instead of assisting in this development of the law themselves, they have taken the view that all major changes should be left to Parliament. This view is, of course, perfectly consistent with their judicial duty; but it does mean that those who are in the best position to know in which way the law should develop are deliberately refraining from developing it. On the other hand, some judges make a point of including in their reasons for judgment whole paragraphs calling the attention of the legislature to the need for reform of the law on the aspect then before the court.

Criticisms of conservatism on the bench do not imply a call for radical change. If judges could disregard the existing law and decide in accordance with their personal feelings the coherent structure of the law would be lost. Even the radical judge's own decision could be overturned at any time by another judge whose feelings were different. Members of the public need to be able to rely on the law: if they cannot, long-term planning becomes almost impossible.

---

1   *Parker v British Airways Board* [1982] QB 1004 Donaldson LJ (later Lord Donaldson of Lymington MR) at 1017.

The effectiveness of the law-making process as a whole

It is easy to point to aspects of our law-making process which fall short of the high level of effectiveness which is in the best interests of the community. It is more difficult to suggest means of achieving that level. Moreover, the fact that criticism can be made of the law-making process does not of itself mean that the process lacks effectiveness. If our law-making process lacked effectiveness, our community would disintegrate. The very fact that our community is continuing, the fact that the opportunities for the individual within the community are increasing, the fact that the individual can gain greater skills and greater home comforts than could have been gained half a century ago, and the fact that our police forces are comparatively small in number, all point to the fact that we have an effective law-making process. The real question is whether our law-making process could, and should, be more effective.

On the whole, the laws which our law-making process produces are accepted by the community. Indeed, it has been said of subordinate legislation in general that it is made for at most 5% of the people: the other 95% will do the right thing anyway. That statement has drawn forth the comment: 'Except when driving a motor car!'

Our law-making process would be more effective if it produced greater consistency. The disparity between penalties for varying offences shows that there has been a failure to review the multiplicity of criminal offences and penalties and a failure to relate the penalties for new offences to the penalties for existing ones. The average citizen, however, is unlikely to carry out the research needed to discover those disparities, and the law is therefore effective despite them. This is fortunate, for the great bulk of legislation and of subordinate legislation that is erupting today makes the pursuit of consistency very difficult.

Probably the greatest criticisms that can be made of our law-making process are that too much of the law is unintelligible to that average citizen whose duty it is to obey it, and the law is too difficult for the average citizen to discover. At least, unlike countries with a less stable form of government, our community does have a general confidence in the law-making process. It is important to the welfare of the community that that confidence be maintained.

CHAPTER 10

THE LEGAL PROFESSION

Solicitors

Historically there are two branches to the legal profession: solicitors and barristers. To these must be added, of course, the judges. A person who wishes to litigate, or to have legal business transacted, or to get advice on the law, should turn to a solicitor. The solicitor will handle the legal side of transactions ranging from the purchase of a house to complex company takeovers; the solicitor may arrange loans, draw up contracts for commercial dealings, handle clients' applications to government bodies, incorporate companies, draw up wills, and advise on taxation matters, amongst many others. Although a solicitor may be likened to a general practitioner in the field of medicine, many solicitors are specialists in their own fields. Some solicitors are experts of national and some of international standing.

Barristers

The principal justification for the existence of the separate branch of barristers (known collectively as the Bar) is the expertise which the Bar develops. Just as one medical practitioner will refer a client to another for his or her opinion, so also a solicitor will refer a client to a barrister. The barrister has the advantage of not being subjected to the pressure of administration and day-to-day affairs of a solicitor's office, and therefore has more time available to carry out the wide range of reading which is essential in many branches of the law. The barrister, too, is required to develop an expertise in the presentation of cases before courts.

Queen's Counsel

A Queen's Counsel (also referred to as One of Her Majesty's Counsel) is a barrister who has attained eminence at the Bar and taken 'silk'. Queen's Counsel enjoy precedence within their profession, and it is from their ranks that judges are usually chosen.

Specialisation

There was a time when every lawyer was expected to be able to advise upon any branch of the law. Indeed, save in the more specialised courts, it is still expected that every judge will be able to hear and decide every type of case. However, the rapidly growing complexities of life have compelled specialisation within the legal profession as well as within numerous other professions upon which the community depends. In England there has long been specialisation within the courts themselves, the High Court of Justice sitting in divisions whose work is devoted to particular branches of the law. In more recent years, the English Bar has developed groups within it known as specialist Bars; and, if a barrister who is being considered for appointment as a Queen's Counsel at the English Bar 'is a member of a specialist Bar, such as the planning or revenue or ecclesiastical law Bars, the Lord Chancellor would ... consult its leader' before deciding whether or not the barrister should be granted such an appointment.[1]

---

1 (1979) 53 ALJ 686.

CHAPTER 11

THE HANDLING OF DISPUTES WITHIN THE LEGAL SYSTEM

How disputes can arise

Disputes between the members of a community are inevitable. It is natural when there are two sides to a dispute for each party to it to see himself or herself as being in the right, and the other party as being in the wrong. Neither is impartial; and it is vital, if both sides are to accept a decision upon the dispute, that the person or body deciding is seen by everyone as being impartial. It is frequently said that 'justice must not only be done but be seen to be done'.

Before the growth of the modern State disputes were mainly between private individuals. Under the medieval system of holding land the fields were divided into strips, and from time to time they were left to lie fallow so that the soil could recover its fertility. During this period it was easy for the markers between strips owned by different persons to become lost or displaced. Disputes were very likely to arise over this matter, since loss of land threatened the livelihood of a man and his family. In medieval times, too, the development of travelling fairs led to commercial disputes between people, the feudal system led to disputes between a man and his overlord, and the claims of the Church led to disputes between the Church authorities and those whom they claimed to be subject to them. The greater complexity of life today gives a much greater scope for disputes. Even in biblical times some men were known for dangerous driving, but the advent of the motor car has given such individuals much greater scope; and, with the increased crowding of our roads, the opportunity for disputes between individuals has increased enormously. The increase in the complexity of modern commerce and industry, and the reliance by many firms upon a chain of suppliers to get the goods they need to them, has led to the possibility of a chain of litigation. The increasing complexity of life naturally means that there are more things that can go wrong, and more people who may be affected, with the result that litigation, also, has increased.

From the earliest times there have been disputes between the individual and the State in the criminal law field; and, as the State developed, there have been disputes in the non-criminal (that is, civil) side of law also. The modern State takes a much wider role in regulating the affairs of its citizens than occurred in previous centuries. This has greatly increased the opportunity for conflict, and therefore for litigation. In early times, whilst such disputes might arise, it was not possible for a citizen to sue the King 'in his own courts'; nowadays, if the government is depriving a citizen of rights (for example, to unemployment relief) that citizen may sue the government and demand redress.

Even as late as the reign of Henry VIII a monarch was able to dispossess a powerful landowner without the landowner having any effective legal redress against the King; by comparison, in the 20th century there have been many cases of successful challenges to compulsory purchase by individuals whose land was proposed to be taken by a government authority. In Tudor times it would have been unthinkable, but in the 20th century landowners have challenged the compulsory purchase of their lands even though the relevant Secretary of State or minister had given approval to the compulsory purchase order under the Act. Upon such a challenge it has been held that:

> the court would be empowered to quash a compulsory purchase order made and confirmed ... if it could be said that there was no evidence upon which the minister could conclude that the acquisition was reasonably necessary for the statutory purpose.[1]

In another case the Court of Appeal quashed a compulsory purchase order because 'the minister had no sufficient material upon which to reach the decision which he did reach',[2] and therefore 'it follows that he acted [beyond the powers conferred by] the section and that his decision is one which should not be permitted to stand'.[3] A compulsory purchase order can be struck down if 'the true purpose of the acquisition was some ulterior purpose not authorised by the statute'.[4] The Court of Appeal has even held that a compulsory purchase order may be held invalid because 'the financial implications of the decision for the property owner must always be relevant'.[5] How far indeed has the common law grown, and how Henry VIII's actions would be treated by the courts today!

In medieval society questions of wages and conditions were settled by the various guilds – such matters were settled within the trade itself and did not ordinarily come before the courts. In 20th-century England such matters generally involve disputes between unions and employers, and they are settled under government authority by those appointed by the government to decide such disputes. Not only do such disputes involve trade unions and employers: government itself may be involved.

There may also be disputes over legislation or subordinate legislation made by the European Community but which introduces factors that are not acceptable to the United Kingdom. Disputes may also be involved (and are likely to arise increasingly in the future) over directives issued by the European Community. Those disputes must be decided upon, not by the English, Scottish or Northern Irish judges, but by the European Court – a court that does not have a doctrine of precedent, leaving each case to be decided without that important benefit.

Disposing of a dispute without a court decision

One method of ending a dispute in one's favour is the method of self-help. If, for example, someone has built a fence onto a neighbour's property, that neighbour

---

1   *Bass Charrington (North) Ltd v Minister of Housing and Local Government* (1970) 22 P&CR 31 at 36.

2   *Coleen Properties Ltd v Minister of Housing and Local Government* [1971] 1 WLR 433, Buckley LJ at 439.

3   *Coleen Properties Ltd v Minister of Housing and Local Government* [1971] 1 WLR 433, Buckley LJ at 439.

4   *Loweth v Minister of Housing and Local Government* (1970) 22 P&CR 125, Bridge J (later Lord Bridge of Harwich) at 133.

5   *Victoria Square Property Co Ltd v Southwark London Borough Council* [1978] 1 WLR 463, Bridge LJ (later Lord Bridge of Harwich) at 474.

may tear down the fence. This method has two disadvantages: first, the person who resorts to self-help may have a mistaken view of rights (and will therefore be liable in damages for the harm caused by tearing the fence down); second, the opponent may resort to self-help also. If both sides resort to self-help, physical conflict may result. An example of self-help that would occur more frequently than the tearing down of a fence is the cutting off of that part of a tree which hangs over onto a neighbour's property: rather than taking the neighbour to court, the landowner whose property the branches overhang can choose to cut off those branches at the property boundary (and may do so without even giving notice to the owner of the trees provided that there is no trespass on that person's land in the course of cutting the branches).[6]

Another method by which a dispute can be disposed of without a court decision is, before or after instituting legal proceedings, abandoning the claim. Thereafter there is no dispute because the other party to the dispute (except as to costs) has succeeded.

Conciliation or mediation is a method of dispute settlement which involves bringing in a mediator. The mediator discusses the matter in dispute with both parties and attempts to bring them to an agreement. The mediator does not have power to force the parties into an agreement: mediation is persuasion, not decision.

Arbitration is a method of dispute settlement in which an arbitrator (selected either by the parties, by a court, or by a person nominated by the parties) considers the matter in dispute and makes a decision binding on both parties. Arbitration is commonly resorted to in order to achieve settlement of commercial disputes. It is used in the expectation that it will be quicker than litigation before a court. For this expectation the court system has only itself to blame. Commercial cases need to be disposed of quickly; yet they are subject to the long delays to which other cases in the court system are exposed. The arbitration may be conducted before one arbitrator, two arbitrators, or three. Each party may appoint its own arbitrator, with those arbitrators (or someone else such as the president of some professional body) selecting the third arbitrator who is known as an 'umpire'. The idea is that the arbitrator will be somebody with specialised knowledge and experience in the particular field to which the dispute relates. In point of fact, the experience is that arbitration is often slower and more expensive than litigation before the courts. It has the disadvantage of involving many technicalities in relation to the extent of the control exercised over arbitrators by the court; and it is by no means unlikely that a complex arbitration will involve a hearing and determination by an arbitrator, the reference of the arbitrator's award to the court, the setting aside of that award by that court, and consequent further consideration (and probably further hearing) by the arbitrator. Many lawyers today advise their clients not to agree to contracts which have clauses requiring arbitration instead of litigation. What is really needed is a system which will give speedy decisions in cases which would otherwise go to arbitration (indeed, there is a need to speed up the whole system of litigation).

---

6   *Lemmon v Webb* [1895] AC 1.

The issue of a writ to commence court proceedings does not necessarily mean that those proceedings will result in a court decision. Many cases are settled before the court hears the matter at all. Others are settled after the beginning of the trial but before a decision is handed down by the judge. A settlement involves an agreement by the parties to end the dispute on terms which have been agreed to by both sides. It is common for a settlement to occur actually at the court door; parties have begun to realise the full cost of such proceedings, and to take a more realistic view of their prospects. Contrary to the idea that is held by many that lawyers encourage litigation, the legal profession in fact plays a major part in achieving settlements. It is the function of a lawyer to take an objective view of the client's case and to weigh up objectively the prospects of success and of failure. Whereas the client is emotionally involved in the case, the lawyer is not; and it is essential that the lawyer must not be emotionally involved if he or she is to give the best advice to the client. Objective advice, with a dispassionate stating of the favourable and adverse points and the likely result, frequently enables the lawyers for the two parties to bring them into agreement. As every lawyer knows, it is often in the interests of both parties to achieve a settlement, thereby saving themselves considerable legal costs.

Another way in which settlement of a case can occur is by the judge hearing the case realising that the costs of litigation in the particular case will be disproportionate to the result, or that bitterness will be engendered by continuing the litigation. Many a judge has persuaded the parties to apply common sense to their dispute instead of fighting it out to the bitter end.

Judges, magistrates, and justices

The courts at the bottom of the judicial hierarchy are the magistrates' courts. The title of the court may be misleading. Such a court may be presided over by a magistrate, it may be presided over by a magistrate and a number of justices of the peace, or it may be presided over by justices of the peace without a magistrate.

Usually the chairman of a tribunal has no security of tenure. The fact that that appointment can be terminated by the government (by contrast with a judge who holds office until retiring age unless removed from office by an address of both Houses of Parliament, and then only for misconduct) does expose the chairman of a tribunal to the risk of pressure being exerted by the authority responsible for recommending reappointment.

Judges of all courts of county court status and higher are qualified members of the legal profession and are required by statute to have had a specified minimum length of experience as practising members of that profession.

The jurisdiction of the courts

A magistrates' court has jurisdiction in both criminal and civil cases. In both instances its jurisdiction is a limited one. It cannot, for example, try the more serious cases of criminal offences such as treason, murder or rape. Although there are some crimes in respect of which the accused can elect to be tried by a judge and jury on the one hand or by a magistrates' court on the other, generally speaking the crimes triable by a magistrates' court are those which Parliament has regarded as the less important crimes. There is, however, no clear test apparent from the legislation for determining whether a particular offence should be placed within the jurisdiction of a magistrates' court. Whilst in most cases any fine that can be imposed by a magistrates' court is a comparatively small one, in tax prosecutions and environment prosecutions the magistrates' court may impose a fine amounting to many thousands of pounds.

The county court is also a court which has both a criminal and a civil jurisdiction, and both its criminal and civil jurisdictions are limited. It can try all but a few of the most serious criminal cases (such as treason, murder, and certain types of conspiracies). Like a magistrates' court, the amount of its civil jurisdiction is limited.

Disposing of a civil dispute by judicial decision

In its civil jurisdiction a court has power to strike out legal proceedings as not disclosing a cause of action. There are circumstances in which the intending plaintiff can only validly bring legal proceedings if certain requirements are complied with; and, if there is a failure to comply with those requirements, the legal proceedings must be struck out. Similarly, if the plaintiff alleges a breach of what is not recognised by the law as a right at all, the action must be struck out. An action will also have to be struck out if the plaintiff lacks legal standing: an unincorporated club, for example, is not what the law recognises as a 'person' and therefore cannot institute legal proceedings as a club (its position, therefore, being in sharp contrast with that of a club which is incorporated or with that of a private individual). An action may also be struck out by a court if the plaintiff has failed to pursue it with reasonable promptness: in such a case it is said to be struck out for want of prosecution (the term 'prosecution' here being used not in a criminal sense but in the sense of proceeding with the case).

One order which a court may make in resolving a dispute brought before it is an order of dismissal. It may dismiss the plaintiff's claim on the ground that the plaintiff has not proved the case. Another order which a court may make in a civil dispute is an order that the defendant pay damages to the plaintiff (there may also be cross-proceedings as a result of which the plaintiff may be ordered to pay damages to the defendant in the particular circumstances).

A court may dispose of civil proceedings before it by making an order requiring the defendant to do certain specified things, or prohibiting the defendant from doing those things. A common form of order in this regard is known as the injunction. There is the interim injunction granted as a matter of urgency to preserve the existing position until such time as the defendant can place his or her case before the court; there is the interlocutory injunction designed to maintain the existing position until the action can be heard in full; and there is the permanent injunction which, as its name indicates, is granted after a full hearing of the case and continues indefinitely. An injunction may be a mandatory injunction requiring certain things to be done, or it may be an injunction prohibiting certain things being done.

Orders requiring certain things to be done or prohibiting them from being done can also be obtained by means of what are known as the prerogative writs. Probably the best known of these writs is the writ of *mandamus*, an order commanding a person or body to perform a legal duty. Another prerogative writ, the writ of prohibition, as its name indicates, prohibits a person or body from doing what is specified in it.

The writ of *quo warranto* is a means by which a superior court can try the question as to whether or not a person claiming to hold a particular public office does so validly; and, if the court finds that the person is not validly in that office, it can require him or her to vacate it. *Certiorari* is a prerogative writ enabling a superior court to review the proceedings in a lower court or tribunal so as to correct any error of law. *Habeas corpus* is a writ enabling a prisoner to obtain a decision by a superior court as to whether or not the prisoner is correctly imprisoned and, if wrongly imprisoned, an order that he or she be released.

A very useful order that can be made to dispose of a civil dispute is a declaratory order which is an order declaring what the rights of the parties are. Such an order does not of itself compel anyone to do anything, but it is unusual for the parties not to accept and abide by it.

It is normal for the party who loses legal proceedings to be ordered to pay costs to the successful party (in some cases there are statutory provisions restricting or preventing this). The order for costs is seldom for the full costs incurred by the successful party. Full costs are only payable if the order is for costs on what is known as a solicitor and own client basis. The usual order for costs is what is known as an order for party and party costs, the extent of those costs usually being only a portion of the costs incurred by the successful party.

CHAPTER 12

THE TRIAL OF A CIVIL CASE

Pleadings

The formal documents which bring the matter before a court are naturally less formal in those courts which are on the lower rungs of the hierarchy of courts. In the superior courts there is a formal system of an exchange of documents between the parties and the filing of those documents in the court, usually substantially in advance of the hearing.

There are some matters in the superior courts which may be commenced by means of a document known as a summons, a document which calls upon the other party to appear before the court on a specified date and to show cause why the order sought in the summons should not be made. The summons must be supported by an affidavit (which is a typed statement made on oath setting out the facts relied upon by the party which has caused the summons to be issued). In some circumstances instead of a summons the initiating document is known as a notice of motion, and that document also must be supported by an affidavit. As an alternative to an affidavit, however, the law has made provision for those who have a religious objection to taking an oath; and, accordingly, both summonses and notices of motion may be supported by a documentary statement of the facts on affirmation instead of on oath.

In most cases that are brought before the superior courts the matter starts, not with a summons or a notice of motion, but with a writ. A writ is a formal document issued by an officer of the superior court. It contains a brief statement of the cause of action. The plaintiff has to cause the writ to be served upon the defendant. The defendant then has a limited period within which to file a document with the court indicating an intention to defend the action. This document is known as an 'appearance'. If the defendant fails to file an appearance, the plaintiff may bring the matter before the court for judgment in the absence of the defendant. In certain types of actions the plaintiff may automatically obtain judgment against the defendant in default of appearance without a formal trial of the action.

The writ (or, more properly, what is known as the endorsement on the writ) as already noted sets out in short form what the cause of action relied upon by the plaintiff is. However, a superior court requires a much more detailed statement of the facts relied upon by the plaintiff before the matter can go to trial. That statement is set out in a document known as a statement of claim. It does not set out the evidence, but it does set out in short numbered paragraphs what the relevant facts relied upon by the plaintiff are, and at the end of it there are set out the orders which the plaintiff seeks. The statement of claim may be delivered with the writ, or the plaintiff may choose to deliver it to the defendant after the defendant has entered an appearance.

A defendant who wishes to contest the action is under a duty to respond to the statement of claim by delivering to the plaintiff a document known as a 'defence'. The defence must set out in short numbered paragraphs what the defendant says to each of the paragraphs in the statement of claim. The defendant must admit or deny each of the allegations in the statement of claim; and, if relying on facts that do not appear in the statement of claim, they must be set out in the defence.

There are circumstances in which the defendant may contend that it has a claim against the plaintiff. This can perhaps most readily be seen in the case of a motor accident involving two vehicles. The driver of one of the vehicles may issue a writ against the other claiming damages. The other driver, if claiming the plaintiff was in the wrong, will not only deliver a defence but will include in the defence what is known as a counterclaim which is in effect a statement of claim for an action against the plaintiff but, because it is incorporated in the document known as the defence, it avoids the necessity of bringing separate proceedings. The plaintiff, if wishing to contest the counterclaim, must deliver a defence to it.

The party to whom a defence is delivered must examine it to see whether it is desirable to contest any of the facts alleged in it that did not appear in the statement of claim (or in the counterclaim) and, if desiring to contest them, setting that out, together with any other facts that are relied on in relation to those facts, in yet a further document known as a reply. If no reply is delivered (or, if the pleadings in the particular case include a reply, then when that reply is delivered), the pleadings are said to be 'closed'. It is then the responsibility of the plaintiff to collate the pleadings and file them with the court.

Interrogatories

There are various types of proceedings in the superior courts in which it becomes desirable to deliver to the other party what are known as interrogatories. Interrogatories are a set of questions delivered by one party to the other. They ask questions about the facts of the case which the other party is obliged to answer (provided, of course, that the questions are relevant and proper). The answers are required to be given on oath or by affirmation, and the party delivering the interrogatories can use all or any of those answers as part of that party's evidence at the hearing of the case. Interrogatories can only be used in civil cases.

Discovery

This procedure, also, is available only in civil cases. A party who is asked to give discovery must make a statement on oath or by affirmation as to all relevant documents formerly, but no longer, in that party's possession, and also all relevant documents of which it had but no longer has possession and where those documents currently are and in whose possession they currently are. That party can be required to allow the other party to inspect and take copies of those documents. The party giving discovery is protected in respect of certain documents which are known as privileged documents (such, for example, as instructions to one's own lawyers).

Interlocutory proceedings

A court may have to deal with certain aspects of a case before the case comes on for trial. For example, the defendant may complain that the statement of claim does not give sufficient information; and, in those circumstances, an application to the plaintiff for further particulars having failed, application may be made to the court to order further particulars of the statement of claim. The same opportunity is available in respect of the reply, and is available to the plaintiff in respect of the defence. Insufficiency of answers to interrogatories, and insufficiency of discovery, can also lead to a court determination of these preliminary matters. All determinations which the court is called upon to make prior to the actual hearing of the case are known as interlocutory.

An important interlocutory proceeding is an application for an interlocutory injunction. This is an injunction operative until the hearing of the case and restraining the other party to the case proceeding with what that other party was doing or was intending to do. This is different to an interim injunction (which is an urgent injunction granted before hearing the other side so as to retain the existing position until the other side can be heard). Interlocutory orders of this nature are necessary to prevent irreparable damage being done pending the hearing of the action.

Representation of the parties

Any individual who is a party to court proceedings has the choice of arguing the case personally before the court or of being represented by a trained lawyer (save in those instances in which Parliament has prohibited legal representation).

A corporation does not have the choice that is available to the individual. A corporation can only put its case before a court by engaging a lawyer to do so for it (in those courts and tribunals in which Parliament has prohibited lawyers from appearing, the corporation would have to appoint an agent to appear for it). The fact that a corporation is put in a different position to an individual may at first sight appear curious. However, upon analysis, it is found to have a very good logical basis. The corporation itself, of course, cannot possibly come before the court because it has no physical existence. The idea of a corporation (such, for example, as Barclays Bank plc) physically appearing in the courtroom is an impossibility. It may be asked, however, why the company cannot authorise one of its directors to appear for it. The answer is that a lay person cannot be authorised to appear for a private individual: the private individual as a party must appear in person or must engage a lawyer. On the same principle as the private individual, the company must engage a lawyer because it cannot put its argument in person. The advantages of having the case argued by a skilled lawyer are set out in Chapter 14.

The hearing

A civil case in a magistrates' court may be heard by a magistrate, by a magistrate together with justices of the peace, or by justices of the peace (in some instances Parliament requires the case to be heard by a magistrate without justices of the peace). From the county court upwards the case will be heard by a judge.

The way in which a case is presented before a court is for each party to present its case in turn. The lawyer 'opens' the case (that is, explains to the court what the case is about and outlines the evidence that the witnesses for that party will give). Each witness for that party is then called in turn and gives evidence either on oath or, if that witness has a religious objection to the taking of an oath, by affirmation. The evidence given to that stage of the trial is known as evidence-in-chief. Each witness, on completing evidence-in-chief, may be cross-examined by the lawyer for the defendant: cross-examination is a series of questions put to the witness in order to test the evidence and either to establish additional facts or obtain alterations in one or more respects, or to gain admissions that some or all of that witness's evidence-in-chief was wrong. There is a famous example of successful cross-examination in which the plaintiff claimed that, as a result of an accident, he could only lift his arm a certain distance. The barrister who was cross-examining him for the defendant asked him in sympathetic tones to demonstrate to the court just how high he could lift his arm. The plaintiff, with a great deal of obvious effort, raised it part way (a little below the shoulder level). The barrister for the defendant, very sympathetically, asked if he could possibly raise it a little further. With a great deal of further effort the plaintiff managed to raise it very slightly further. The barrister for the defendant then asked: 'How high could you lift your arm before the accident?' The plaintiff immediately raised his arm right up above his head!

After cross-examination has been completed the lawyer for the party whose witness has been cross-examined then has the right to ask that witness further questions (known as re-examination). Questions in re-examination are confined to matters arising out of the cross-examination and are intended to clarify anything which was unclear in the answers given during cross-examination or which may have been incomplete when given during cross-examination.

The judge, of course, has the right to ask questions of a witness at any stage of the proceedings. It is usual for a judge only to ask those questions which he or she feels have not been asked by the barristers for the parties and which would assist in determining the case, and it is an established principle that the judge must not ask so many questions as to disrupt the presentation of the case by the parties.

The system of evidence-in-chief, cross-examination and re-examination of course relates to evidence given orally. Evidence may also be given (or, to use the technical term, adduced) in written form. This is known as documentary evidence, and may be given in addition to or in substitution for oral evidence. There are some cases which are tried solely on documentary evidence. For example, a case in which all that the court is called upon to do is to interpret a contract may not involve the giving of any oral evidence at all: the contract can be placed before the court by agreement, or it can be annexed to an affidavit (being then what is known as an exhibit to that affidavit). There is an increasing tendency today to require the evidence of expert witnesses to be given in typed form, and to be exchanged between the parties and filed with the court in advance of the hearing; the expert witness giving evidence in that way can supplement that evidence orally, and is of course subject to cross-examination not only upon that oral supplementing of evidence but upon the typed statement itself.

The standard of proof in a civil case

The standard of proof in a civil case is different from that in a criminal case. The standard of proof in a civil action is proof on the balance of probabilities. The onus of proof of particular issues is on the party raising the particular issue. The general onus of proof is on the plaintiff.

The decision

If the case was one heard by a judge and jury, the decision upon the facts must be made by the jury; the decision upon the law must be made by the judge. In all other cases the judge (or, in a magistrates' court, the magistrate or justices of the peace as the case may be) decides both the facts and the law.

Enforcement of the decision in a civil case

The various orders which a court may make are considered in Chapter 11. In the present chapter we consider how those orders are enforced. There would, of course, be no need for enforcement if all parties obeyed all orders made by courts. Unfortunately, some people do not obey court orders. When that happens, the law would become a laughing stock if there were no effective means of enforcing the orders the court has made. The law, of course, does provide such means.

If the court order was one requiring a party to make a payment to the other party, it may be enforced by what is known as 'distress'. This is a procedure which involves a court officer physically seizing goods owned by that party and, if necessary, selling them and paying the party entitled to the money out of the proceeds of the sale. This is expensive for the party whose goods have been so seized because goods sold in that fashion are not likely to attain their ordinary second hand value, let alone their replacement value, and that party also has to pay the charges of the court official for carrying out the seizure and sale. Even if the matter does not proceed as far as the sale of the goods, the party whose goods are seized must pay the court official's charge for the seizure before the goods can be regained.

If the court order is one requiring a party to do a particular thing, or is an order prohibiting doing it, and that party acts in breach of that order (that is, by failing to do what the court has required, or by doing what the court has prohibited), the court order can be enforced against him or her by imprisonment. Failure to do what the court order requires or doing what it prohibits is said to be contempt of court. A party who is in contempt of court can be sent to gaol for an unlimited period of time until the day comes when that party is prepared to come back before the court and to undertake to the court to comply with its order. When that undertaking has been given and the order has been complied with, that party is said to have 'purged his [or her] contempt'. If the court order was one requiring the party to transfer property and there is a refusal to do so, there is not only the procedure by way of contempt but the court may direct someone else to transfer the property on that party's behalf.

CHAPTER 13

THE TRIAL OF A CRIMINAL CASE

Is what has occurred a crime?

Conduct may cause great annoyance to others, and may be regarded as morally harmful, without being a crime. For example, prostitution in itself (as opposed to living off the earnings of prostitution, and soliciting in the streets for customers) has never been a crime in our society. In Iran today, however, it is a crime carrying the most serious penalties: flogging for both the man and the woman and, if the man happens to be married, death for the woman instead of a flogging.

In order to constitute a crime, conduct must be in breach of the criminal law. Most of the criminal offences today are set out in Acts of Parliament or in subordinate legislation, but there are also common law offences. Some crimes (in particular, the more serious ones) require a particular intention on the part of the criminal. For instance, in order to commit murder a person must intend either to kill or to inflict grievous bodily harm, or alternatively must know that conduct might lead to death or grievous bodily harm and continue with it regardless. An accidental killing is not murder, and neither is self-defence (provided that the force used is not excessive in the circumstances), nor is provocation sufficient to reduce it from murder to manslaughter.

There are circumstances in which the necessary intent cannot be formed. The law holds that a child under the age of 10 cannot form the intent to commit any crime. From that age until the age of 14 it has to be proved by the prosecution that the child is capable of forming a guilty intention. Insanity precludes the forming of the relevant intention, whether the insane person be child or adult. Drink or drugs, if they have the effect of preventing the offender from knowing what he or she is doing, or knowing that what he or she is doing is wrong, also prevent the forming of the relevant intention (drink or drugs, in themselves, do not establish this: it is the offender's lack of knowledge which is vital and which must be proved on his or her behalf).

Many offences created by Act of Parliament or by subordinate legislation do not require a guilty intention. Today, Parliament and those making subordinate legislation under its authority are increasingly ready to create offences which are committed without any guilty knowledge: for example, a butcher is guilty of the offence of selling adulterated sausage meat even if not in the shop at the time that the sausage meat was prepared and not even in the shop at the time that an employee sold the sausage meat. The aim in that particular example, is, of course, to compel the employer to make sure that the employees obey the law; but in many other examples of statutory offences, or of offences created by subordinate legislation, the objective is to create offences of strict liability so as to achieve compliance with the law without any question of an intermediary such as an employee. There is cause for concern in the growing number of offences of strict liability. There are so many offences today that a person may commit without any knowledge of breaking the law, and the difficulty of knowing what the law is (particularly criminal offences established by subordinate legislation) emphasises the importance of this matter.

Investigation of offences

It is not only the police who are entitled to investigate the commission of crimes. They, of course, have a major role to play; but departmental inspectors and officers of statutory authorities play a major part in relation to the investigation of breaches of subordinate legislation and, in some cases, of statutory offences. Crimes can also be investigated by such persons as security guards and store detectives, and they can be investigated by private citizens injured by the commission of the offence. It is obvious, for example, that, if theft is occurring from a company, the management will be likely to either investigate the matter itself or call in somebody else to do so (whether police or otherwise). There is no restriction on who may investigate an offence, although there are restrictions on the methods which may be used in doing so. The mere fact that a crime has been committed does not allow the investigator to go outside the law. Subject to statutory exceptions, premises may only be searched if a search warrant is first obtained. Customs officers have wide powers to search the person, but other investigators are normally allowed to do this only after arrest.

The extent to which an individual is obliged to answer police questions

The press often reports euphemistically that an individual is 'helping the police with enquiries' or has been taken to the police station for questioning. The police have no general right to require this sort of help before arrest; and, indeed, the suspect in most circumstances has a right to remain silent (although there are circumstances in which this is not true, or in which silence will tell against the silent one).

Subject to any legislation extending their right to question, the police may question a suspect without warning the suspect of a suspect's rights until such time as they have decided that the suspect has indeed committed an offence. At that point they are required to warn the accused (up to that point the suspect, not the accused) that he or she is not obliged to say anything and that anything he or she says may be put in writing and used in evidence against him or her. The accused may, of course, by this stage have made all the admissions which are necessary to prove the case against him or her. If such a warning is not given, the answers obtained may still be used in court; but the judge has the power, in the public interest, to exclude evidence which has been improperly obtained:

No doubt in a criminal case the judge always has a discretion to disallow evidence if the strict rules of admissibility would operate unfairly against an accused.[1]

---

1   *Kurama v The Queen* [1955] AC 197, Lord Goddard CJ at 204.

There are certain offences in respect of which Parliament has provided that it is for the accused to provide an explanation (for example, to provide a reasonable explanation for the accused's presence in suspicious circumstances). In those circumstances silence is likely to tell against the accused at trial.

The right to prosecute

Unless a particular statute specifically limits this right in respect of a particular offence, any citizen may prosecute for an offence of a public nature.

The right to a fair trial

Under our system of law every accused has the right to a fair trial. That trial must be conducted by a judicial officer and not simply by a member of the executive or police. It is a basic principle of law that no person may be judge in their own cause: this applies not merely to prevent one of the parties in a civil case deciding it in that party's own favour, but also to prevent the police (who, by bringing the accused to trial, have already shown their belief in guilt) from judging the guilt of the accused conclusively.

In most serious cases the accused has a right to trial by judge and jury. Of course, if the accused elects to plead guilty, the accused is dealt with by a judge without a jury because the plea of guilty amounts to admitting all the facts necessary to constitute the offence.

It is a fundamental principle of law that justice must not only be done but be seen to be done. This principle has been repeatedly emphasised by the courts. For example, in the Court of Appeal Lawton LJ, who was delivering the joint reasons for judgment of that court, said: 'It is ... one of the principles of the administration of justice in this country that not only should justice be done ... but it must appear to be done.'[2]

The press and the public are normally admitted to the courtroom where civil or criminal actions are being heard. This is important if justice is to be seen to be done. There are some cases, however, where trials are held and the public is not admitted – for example, for security reasons, in cases in which terrorists are involved. For a different reason, in children's courts the public are not admitted: this is to protect the child from the stigma of conviction.

Bail and remand

The law treats an accused person as innocent until found guilty (except in the case of certain statutory offences). Any formal term of imprisonment as a result of a crime must therefore follow conviction. On the other hand, it is important to prevent accused persons from running away rather than facing their trial; and it is even more important to prevent them from intimidating witnesses against them. There are also crimes of such a nature (such as the case in which a

---

2   *R v Arrowsmith* [1975] 1 All ER 463 at 472.

person is accused of repeated rapes) in which it is vital to hold the accused in custody even before the date of trial so as to protect the public.

When a person has been arrested, a justice of the peace or a magistrate or, on appeal, a judge has the choice of either sending the accused to prison on remand until the date of hearing, or of granting freedom until trial subject to compliance with conditions of bail as imposed in the particular case. When a person is released on bail he or she is required to enter into a written undertaking to appear to face trial, and the person (either alone or with one or more sureties) has to provide a sum of money which will be forfeited upon failure to appear for trial. The money may be lodged in cash, or by leaving the bankbook of the accused or of the surety in the custody of the court. Every accused person held by the police has the right to be brought before a magistrate or justices of the peace in order to apply for bail. The police can of course oppose the granting of bail, and for that purpose they may put evidence before the court relevant to that question.

Summary trial

Summary offences are criminal offences triable summarily (that is, by a magistrates' court). They are to be distinguished from indictable offences, which are criminal offences triable on indictment. Indictable offences are ordinarily tried before a judge and jury; summary offences are tried before a magistrate or justices of the peace sitting without a jury. The distinction does not depend on the seriousness of the offence, but upon the method of trial prescribed by Parliament for that offence. In some cases, the accused has the right to elect to be tried summarily rather than by judge and jury.

The rule against double jeopardy

A person who has been acquitted cannot subsequently be recharged with that same offence. That does not, of course, mean that a person who has been acquitted of, for example, shoplifting can thereafter commit shoplifting with impunity. What it means is that, if a person is charged with having committed the offence of shoplifting on a particular day at a particular place and is acquitted of that charge, that person cannot thereafter be again brought forward for trial in respect of the alleged shoplifting at that time and place.

It is not, however, only the specific offence charged that is covered by the acquittal. A more serious charge may have within it the elements of lesser charges. For example, if a person is charged with murder the jury can acquit of murder but convict of manslaughter. If it acquits altogether, not only is the person acquitted entitled to rely upon that acquittal to prevent any retrial on the murder charge, but is equally entitled to rely upon that acquittal to prevent any further trial in relation to manslaughter. (Also, of course, a person who has already been convicted for a particular offence cannot be tried and punished twice for it.)

Representation

Any accused person has the right to legal representation at trial and, for reasons expressed in the previous chapter, a company must have legal representation if it intends to defend the case. An individual accused may either have a lawyer or defend personally. An accused who is able to pay a lawyer's fees can of course have a choice of lawyer. In normal circumstances, of course, the more experienced the lawyer, the higher the fees. Equally, the more experienced the lawyer is, the greater the benefit the accused is likely to gain from being represented by that lawyer.

Where an accused is unable to pay a lawyer's fees, assistance is available to help that accused obtain legal representation. It is a mark of the fairness of our system of criminal justice that the accused who is without financial means may have the case presented for the defence without cost by a junior barrister or even by the ablest of Queen's Counsel assigned for the purpose.

Even though in prison awaiting trial, the accused's right to representation includes a right to consult with legal advisers. This right is a vital protection to the accused; for, if the legal advisers were unable to speak with the accused and to go through the case with him or her, they would be unable to defend the accused properly at the trial.

Selecting a jury

This topic is dealt with in Chapter 16.

Procedure at the trial

The procedure at a criminal trial can most clearly be seen from the following summary:

(a) If the case is tried by judge and jury, the accused has the right to challenge an unlimited number for cause (until Criminal Justice Act 1988 there was also the right to challenge a limited number of jurors without stating any cause).

(b) Irrespective of the mode of trial the accused is deemed innocent until proven guilty (save in certain limited cases in which the presumption of innocence has been expressly changed by statute).

(c) Save in certain limited cases expressly provided for by statute:

    (i) The burden of proof is on the prosecution;

    (ii) The prosecution has to prove its case beyond reasonable doubt;

    (iii) Unless the character of a police witness is put in issue, or the accused adduces evidence of good character, the accused's prior convictions cannot be referred to until after conviction.

(d) The charge must:

    (i) Give the accused sufficient particulars to know the case to be met;

    (ii) Be served sufficiently far in advance to enable the accused (and the accused's lawyers) to prepare the case.

(e) The trial procedure:

    (i) Is an adversary procedure; and

    (ii) Enables the accused or the legal advisers to cross-examine the prosecution witnesses and to call witnesses for the defence.

(f) The accused is free to give evidence, but is not compelled to do so: the choice is to

    (i) Stay silent; or

    (ii) Make an unsworn statement; or

    (iii) Give evidence.

Deciding the facts and the law

The jury is the sole judge of the facts, and the judge is the sole judge of the law. In the case of a magistrates' court there is of course no jury, and the magistrate or justices of the peace will decide on both fact and law.

CHAPTER 14

THE ADVERSARY SYSTEM

The meaning of the adversary system

The so-called adversary system is a system that is fundamental to the court system as it is known in England, in Australia, and in the other British dominions and colonies. It is the basis of that system that each party has a full and fair opportunity of presenting that party's case to the court or tribunal that has to consider it.

The advantages of the adversary system

In courts, and in those administrative tribunals before which lawyers are entitled to appear for clients, the court or tribunal has the benefit of the long-developed ethical requirements of the legal profession. By those ethical requirements it is firmly established that a lawyer has a duty not only to the client but also to the court (and also a duty to the legal profession). The duty to the court requires the lawyer not to bring forward evidence known to be perjured; and it requires the lawyer to search for and to bring to the court's attention all relevant precedents.[1] The duty to the court is a very important one, and compliance with it is insisted upon by the courts and by the legal profession.

Legal representation before a court or tribunal also gives that court or tribunal the benefit of an argument presented by professional people who have been trained in the presentation of an argument. A reasoned, logical argument confined to what is relevant is far more likely to persuade a court or tribunal than one presented without those characteristics.

The fact that all parties are allowed to have their say, and to challenge the evidence of the opposing party on the points at issue, helps to increase confidence in the legal system. Many people, however, would be too nervous to put their own case; and few would have the experience, the knowledge, or the ability to put their case effectively. They are therefore allowed to put their case through their legal representative. A litigant can appear personally to carry out what would otherwise be a lawyer's duty. The advantages of having legal representation are obvious, and in practice the litigant is well advised to have the benefit of the skilled professionalism which has been the hallmark of the legal profession for many centuries.

Another advantage which the litigant gains by having skilled legal assistance is that of having objective, expert advice. It is the function of a lawyer to be dispassionate: the client is likely to be involved emotionally in the case; the lawyer must not be. For this among other reasons it has often been said that 'he who is his own lawyer has a fool for his client'.

---

1   *Glebe Sugar Refining Co v Trustees of the Port and Harbours of Greenock* [1921] SC HL 72.

On the continent of Europe criminal trials are conducted under the investigative rather than the adversary system: the judge is known as a judge of investigation and he takes an active part in ferreting out the facts rather than acting as an impartial referee. Furthermore, under the investigative system the judge is not (as in our system) a person who has had many years of experience at the Bar handling cases sometimes for one side, sometimes for the other: he is a government official who has been a member of the judiciary since completing his legal training. The judge in an inquisitorial system is both judge and prosecutor.

The adversary system involves less risk than the investigative system of a judge being affected by ideas formulated by him before the whole of the evidence has been obtained; and it gives greater opportunity for counsel than does the investigative system of combating any preconceived ideas the judge may have. There is an element of unfairness to the accused in the investigative system that does not occur in the adversary system. Great care is taken under the British legal system to ensure that, if the accused has previous convictions, they are not disclosed to the jury unless the accused's character is put in issue; but a French trial proceeds on the basis that practically all that there is to know about an accused, whether past or present, is searched out and used by the court.

Disadvantages of the adversary system

Under the adversary system, the parties, rather than the court, decide what evidence is to be brought forward. It may be that there is evidence which neither side desires to bring forward. Under the investigative system the judge may well uncover this evidence and drag it into the light. Under the adversary system this is unlikely to happen, although there are circumstances in which the judge will direct the parties' attention to the desirability of bringing such evidence forward. Since a trial under our system is a contest between two or more parties they are likely between them to bring forward all the evidence that will assist in furthering their respective cases.

It is possible that the adversary system may result in lengthier litigation, but this is unlikely in practice. Counsel on both sides have experience in selecting relevant evidence and are generally unlikely to risk boring the judge and jury by wasting their time. The greatest delays are likely to occur if the parties appear in person. Under the French system (the investigative system) judges are likely to enquire into a case several times over a period. This may well take longer than the proceedings under the adversary system.

In any field of endeavour the person who can pay the fees of the most skilled members of a profession is at a great advantage. For instance, the person who can obtain the services of a specialist will have a better chance of surviving particular diseases. Similarly, in the legal profession, some barristers and solicitors are more skilled than others. The person who obtains the services of the most skilled lawyers has an advantage over a less ably represented opponent.

The adversary system as we know it involves the system of examination-in-chief of witnesses, their cross-examination by the other side, and re-examination by the side which called the witness, as discussed earlier in this book. This system makes it difficult for witnesses to give their evidence in their own way, and may deprive the court of the advantage of the witnesses' natural reactions. A skilful lawyer is often able to put the witness at a disadvantage, or by the questions which are asked to make the witness appear either to be a fool or to draw back from the evidence which he or she had previously given. Of course, the witness may be a fool or a liar, and it is the aim of cross-examination to reveal this fact if it is so. Unfortunately, the same tactics which reveal lies and folly may also confuse an honest person. Many witnesses have never been in court before, and are therefore at a disadvantage. However, it is one of the functions of the judge to prevent unfair treatment of witnesses. This can be done either by asking questions to bring out the truth, or by carefully analysing the evidence by that witness when summing up to the jury, or by preventing the putting of unfair questions or questions asked in an unfair manner.

However fair the adversary system tries to be in practice, there is a popular conception that lawyers can and do mislead the jury. This popular conception is reflected in the Lord Chancellor's song in *Iolanthe*:

> I'll never throw dust in a juryman's eyes (Said I to myself – said I),
> Or hoodwink a judge who is not over-wise (Said I to myself – said I).

Attempts to exclude the legal profession

Lawyers are the heirs to a long tradition of professional responsibility. They are bound by strict standards of ethics, and any serious breach will not merely lead to the disapproval of their fellow members of the profession but is likely to lead to exclusion from the profession altogether and consequent loss of livelihood. Advocates without legal training are not subject to the traditions or the discipline imposed on barristers and solicitors. Consequently, although Parliament from time to time shows an obvious favouring of the lay advocate instead of the lawyer, the risk of abuse of the processes of the court or tribunal and the risk of failing to achieve proper representation and a fair result inevitably increase very considerably. The problem inherent in a system of lay advocates is illustrated by a statement made in the course of a decision by an administrative tribunal:

> We have had occasion before to stress to Mr ... the importance of obtaining accurate instructions from his clients. Any failure to be accurate in this respect in a manner capable of misleading the Tribunal will not be tolerated.

CHAPTER 15

THE RULES OF EVIDENCE

The meaning of evidence

Like so many words, 'evidence' has a number of meanings. We have seen in an earlier chapter that 'charity' means one thing to the person untrained in law and another thing to the lawyer, and that the legal meaning of 'charity' is wider than its meaning in ordinary speech. That is also true of the meaning of 'evidence'. As the Court of Appeal put it:

> In police experience, evidence means information which can be put before a court; and it means that not only to police officers but to the general public, as is shown clearly by one of the meanings given to the word 'evidence' in the *Shorter Oxford English Dictionary*, 3rd edn (1944), p 643 which, under the subheading 'law', defines 'evidence' in these terms: 'Information that is given in a legal investigation, to establish the fact or point in question'. If a police officer, who was trying to understand what the word 'evidence' meant in the Judges' Rules, felt that he ought to turn to a standard legal textbook in case the *Oxford Dictionary* definition was too wide, and he turned to *Phipson on Evidence*, 11th edn (1970), p 2, para 3, he would have found 'evidence' defined as follows: 'Evidence, as used in judicial proceedings, has several meanings. The two main senses of the word are: first, the means, apart from argument and inference, whereby the court is informed as to the issues of fact as ascertained by the pleadings; second, the subject matter of such means.' In the judgment of this court, that is how a police officer would understand these rules.[1]

The different types of evidence

The average person probably thinks of 'evidence' as something spoken by a witness in court. Evidence, however, may take various forms. The two most obvious categories of evidence are oral evidence and documentary evidence. Oral evidence is the evidence which a witness gives by word of mouth in court. Documentary evidence is, as its name suggests, evidence composed of documents placed before the court either by a witness or by the lawyer representing the particular party.

Another type of evidence is referred to by the very confusing name of 'real evidence'. This type of evidence is, for example, a car that has been recovered after being stolen, a gun that has been used to kill, a knife that has been used in an attack, or housebreaking tools found in the possession of the accused. The term 'real' evidence for this type of evidence must not be allowed to cause the wrong impression that oral evidence or documentary evidence is regarded by a court as any less real.

Another classification of evidence is into what are called 'primary evidence' and 'secondary evidence'. Sometimes instead of 'primary' the word used is 'best'. The best, or primary, evidence of a document is the original of that document. Secondary evidence is ordinarily a copy of that document. However,

---

1   *R v Osbourne* [1973] 1 QB 678 at 688.

if a document has been lost or destroyed, it is possible to give oral evidence of the contents of that document. There is a famous example concerning a will. Lord St Leonard's was a highly respected Lord Chancellor of England. He spent a great deal of time drafting and revising his will. He and his sister shared a house. Many an evening he spent discussing the contents of the will with her in detail. When he died, the will could not be found, but she was able to prove the contents of that will by oral testimony.

The purpose of the rules of evidence

The basic purpose of the rules of evidence is to ensure that a case is tried in an orderly and proper manner, and that the facts are ascertained by reference only to material which is of value and which can, if necessary, be properly tested. Even with the safeguards provided by the rules of evidence, there have been notorious miscarriages of justice. In one particularly unfortunate example, a person was convicted of murder (and subsequently hanged) on the sworn oral evidence of a person who was subsequently found to be the actual murderer: the person who was convicted and hanged was in fact innocent of the crime.

Anyone who reads the popular press with a critical eye knows how readily a wrong impression can be created. No matter how carefully and honestly a person may try to give evidence, there is always the risk of that evidence being slanted or mistaken. In one motor accident case there were six witnesses: three gave sworn evidence that one of the cars was going forward at a fast rate, one swore that it was going forward in first gear (and therefore slowly), the fifth swore that it was stationary, whilst the sixth swore that it was going in reverse! The probable explanation is that those whose evidence was mistaken had heard the crash, seen the position of the cars at that point of time, and within seconds their minds had automatically reconstructed what 'must' have happened. In another instance an unidentified police car was driving along a road when an elderly gentleman tripped and fell flat on the side of the roadway. The police driver, thinking quickly, did a U-turn with a squeal of tyres and brakes, and pulled up immediately behind the fallen man so as to prevent him being run over by approaching traffic. The police driver was not even out of the car before a bystander had come up excitedly accusing him of knocking the man down!

The rules of evidence are designed to exclude the more unreliable evidence (there are, of course, very real limits to the extent to which they can achieve that!) and to afford means of testing the evidence that is given.

The exclusion of inadmissible evidence

The test of admissibility of evidence can be very clearly seen by considering the position of an accused person during a criminal trial. The police in the case against the person being prosecuted might have a very strong desire to tell the jury about the accused's long criminal record. In ordinary circumstances, they are not allowed to do so. That is because what is in issue before the court is not whether the accused has had a bad record in the past but whether the person before the court committed the particular crime. However, if the accused attacks the character of the police witnesses (as, for example, by suggesting that they have invented a confession they alleged he or she made), then the police can give evidence of the accused's criminal record because it is relevant to the issue of character – the accused's character as against theirs.

Evaluating evidence

The fact that a person gives oral evidence on oath (or by affirmation) in court does not mean that that evidence has to be accepted. It is the task of the judge (or, if there is a jury, the task of the jury) to weigh up that evidence. It is the function of the lawyer for the other party to test that evidence by cross-examination so that the judge (or jury) may have a proper basis for weighing that evidence. It is seldom, indeed, that two people will have an identical recollection of what has occurred in the past. Human memory has its frailties. Each witness may be telling the truth to the best of his or her ability, but the judge has to decide which is the more correct. The judge may, indeed, decide that one witness is more correct on some aspects and another witness is more correct on others. Obviously, if a party does not adduce available evidence, the failure to adduce it will tell against that party in the weighing of the evidence that is before the court.

Circumstantial evidence

Oral evidence of what the witness saw is direct evidence. There are cases, however, in which direct evidence of a particular fact is not available. It may then be possible to prove the particular issue by the use of what is known as circumstantial evidence – evidence of circumstances that make it probable that a particular state of facts existed. A very good example of the dangers of circumstantial evidence is given in a short story by M Davisson Post, *A Twilight Adventure*:

> 'Well,' replied my uncle, 'what circumstantial evidence proves, depends a good deal on how you get started. It is a somewhat dangerous road to the truth, because all the signboards have a curious trick of pointing in the direction that you are going. Now, a man will never realise this unless he turns around and starts back, then he will see, to his amazement, that the signboards have also turned. But as long as his face is set one certain way, it is of no use to talk to him, he won't listen to you; and if he sees you going the other way, he will call you a fool.'
> 'There is only one way in this case,' said Ward.
> 'There are always two ways in every case,' replied Abner, 'that the suspected person is either guilty or innocent.'[2]

It is small wonder that a leading law dictionary says that:

> As a general principle ... it is true that positive evidence of a fact from credible eye-witnesses is the most satisfactory that can be produced; and the universal feeling of mankind leans to this species of evidence in preference to that which is merely circumstantial.[3]

---

2   *Fifty Famous Detectives of Fiction*, London, Odhams Press Ltd, 333 at 340.
3   *Jowitt's Dictionary of English Law*, 2nd edn, 1977, 345.

Prima facie evidence

Prima facie evidence is evidence that, although not conclusive in itself, can be acted upon and relied upon by the court unless and until contrary evidence is adduced. Acts of Parliament frequently provide for certain evidence to be *prima facie* evidence, and it is important that the right to adduce evidence to rebut that *prima facie* evidence is preserved.

Hearsay evidence

Hearsay evidence is evidence of what the witness was told by somebody else and was so told in the absence of the party against whom the evidence is sought to be given. Because hearsay evidence, from its very nature, cannot be properly tested, it is usually inadmissible.

Judicial notice

A court can take what is known as judicial notice of facts that are so notorious (that is, so well-known) that evidence of them is regarded as unnecessary. It would be a waste of time to have to call evidence to prove to a judge that the court in which he or she sat day after day was in a building fronting a particular street: the judge knows that fact, and it is a fact that is a notorious fact. As an example, a court will take judicial notice of the number of days in any particular month, but it will not take judicial notice of the time at which sunset occurred upon a particular day.[4]

Presumption of accuracy

It is assumed, until contrary evidence is given, that a scientific instrument is accurate.

Refreshing a witness's memory

Just as an examination is a test of a person's memory, so also is the giving of evidence. However, the fact that a person's memory proves insufficient does not necessarily prevent that person from giving evidence. If the witness made a written record of what occurred at the time that it occurred, memory may be 'refreshed' by referring to that written record. To do so, the witness must first give from memory all that he or she can recall, and, having done so, that written record can be used.

A witness cannot refresh memory from a written record made by someone else, even though that witness was present when that written record was made (and, of course, present when the incident occurred which is recorded in that written record). The written record must, of course, be a proper record of what occurred, and not a summary of it. For example, if what is being recorded is a

---

4   *Collier v Nokes* (1849) 2 Car & Kir 1012.

conversation, what is said by each person must be recorded and not merely a summary of the effect of the conversation – such a summary would not be allowed to be used.

Without prejudice letters or conversations

It is important for parties to litigation, or to possible litigation, to be able to have discussions or to conduct correspondence free of the risk that what they say can be used against them. That freedom encourages discussions that can avoid litigation or that can result in settlement of the litigation without it going to court. This freedom is gained if the conversation or the correspondence is expressed to be 'without prejudice'. This type of evidence caused an English solicitor to write:

> Without prejudice letters, you'll generally find,
> Are the most prejudicial and prejudiced kind.[5]

Unless it is expressly stated to the contrary, a reply to a 'without prejudice' letter is itself treated as being without prejudice.

Admissions

An admission is an acknowledgment by a party that something is so or has occurred. The admission may be by express words, or it may be by silence in circumstances in which a response would be expected. The fact that someone admits something to be as they admit it to be does not mean that it is in fact so; but the admission becomes evidence against them of its being so. As Darling J remarked: 'Admissions are mostly made by those who do not know their importance.'[6]

---

5   JPC, *Poetic Justice* at 73.
6   *Scintillae Juris*, 6th edn, 1914, at 59.

CHAPTER 16

THE JURY SYSTEM

The origin of the jury system

The jury system preceded our modern system of courts of law. It can, in fact, be traced back in England to the time of the Anglo-Saxons. There was a custom in those days whereby a man accused of a crime would be acquitted if the necessary number of persons came forward and swore that they believed him to be innocent.

The function of the jury

The function of the jury in a criminal case is ordinarily to decide whether the accused is guilty beyond reasonable doubt. However, the criminal jury may be called upon to decide a preliminary issue, namely whether the person who is accused is mentally fit to plead to the charge.

The function of the jury in a civil case is to decide between the parties on the balance of probabilities and to award damages. It may, however, have a much more limited function. Whether it has that more limited function depends upon the nature of the case and what the parties desire to obtain by way of a jury verdict. The parties may desire to have a jury verdict upon certain questions only, thus establishing the facts, and then argue the legal effect of those facts and the amount (if any) to be awarded before the judge.

Justification for retaining juries in criminal trials

One justification for retaining the use of a jury in a criminal trial is that the jury can act as a barrier between the citizen and the State, its power to acquit the accused giving it a means of dealing effectively with misuse of the power of the State so far as that particular accused is concerned. A comparatively early example is to be found in the acquittal by a jury of the bishops in the reign of James II. Those bishops were prosecuted for seditious libel because they had presented a petition to the King seeking not to have a royal declaration read in churches.[1]

Juries serve as a barometer of the prevailing ideas in the community. For example, in the early part of the 19th century, when it was an offence carrying the death penalty to steal property to the value of £2, juries, in convicting, gave as their verdict that the accused was guilty of stealing a Bank of England £10 note 'to the value of £1.19s.11d' (£1.99). The jury as such a barometer, however, does not always succeed.

The absence of a jury in a totalitarian state is significant. Some totalitarian states have what may be described as mob-trial, a form of 'trial' in which the mob is very easily manipulated by its political masters. In place of the jury as a

---

1   *Seven Bishops' case* (1688) 12 State Tr 183; 87 ER 136.

protective barrier for the individual against the State, the totalitarian State substitutes the mob as a means of advancing the State against the individual.

It is important that the citizens as a whole have confidence in the impartiality of the administration of justice. A court in which the accused has a say in the selection of those by whom that accused is to be tried is far more likely to have the confidence of the accused than one appointed wholly by the State. The fact is that the jury system in criminal trials has not only existed for centuries, but has been and is regarded by the general public as a basic feature of our system of criminal justice. Abandoning it could be seen as a move militating against fairness in the administration of the criminal law. It should be improved, not abolished.

Justification for retaining juries in civil cases

It is often argued against trial by jury that jury verdicts in respect of injuries vary considerably. So they do, but the alternative is a uniformity that tends to crystallise. If that uniformity is achieved by statute, the scale prescribed by the statute is unlikely to be amended frequently and therefore will not keep abreast of the changing value of money.

Not only does the jury system in civil cases provide that flexibility, but it allows the taking into account of individual circumstances that can have no part in a prescribed scale. How can there be a scale, for example, prescribing the amount of damages payable to a girl who is disfigured by motor accident injuries? The extent and the very nature of the disfigurement may vary so much from case to case. Not all disfigurement can be cured by plastic surgery; and the length of time taken in a series of plastic surgery operations coupled with the varying nature of disfigurement in between is something that could hardly be set out in a formalised scale.

The most significant fact about civil juries is that they are obviously wanted as the mode of trial by a substantial number of litigants. A jury in a criminal trial in any court higher than the magistrates' court in the hierarchy of courts is automatic; but, in a civil trial, a jury is only used if one or other of the litigants chooses to have it. The fact that many civil trials continue to be trials by jury speaks for itself.

Criticisms of juries in criminal cases

There are grounds upon which persons may be excused from jury service and there are grounds upon which a person is ineligible to serve on a jury. Consequently, the commonly held view that a jury is composed of a cross-section of the community differs from the reality.

The result of the right to be excused and of certain of the categories of ineligibility, coupled with the jury selection system, is that a jury does not represent a true cross-section of the community. This can perhaps best be seen by considering the method by which juries are in fact selected in criminal cases. When the panel of prospective jurors has assembled in the courtroom and the accused has pleaded not guilty, the names of the prospective jurors are called out individually to give the accused the right to challenge them and the Crown the more limited right of standing them aside.

Although there are some persons who are called for jury service on several occasions within a comparatively short period it is not usual to find anyone who has served on more than two or three juries in a lifetime. Jurors, therefore, are unlikely to be familiar with court procedure (worse, they may have seen American television films which show a completely different procedure). There is no provision for the court procedure to be explained to them in advance, and what happens in practice is that it unfolds before them progressively. The jurors, who may well be unused to considering arguments extending over perhaps days (in some cases even longer) are not even provided with pen and paper, and are not provided with a copy of the transcript of evidence (this is the official record of evidence, a copy of which is made available to the judge and to each of the barristers in the case, but not to the jury).

There are cases in which jurors are unable to agree upon their verdict. This puts the State and the accused to the expense (and the accused to the anxiety) of a second, or even a third or fourth, trial. There are also cases in which it is difficult to obtain a fair trial by jury. This can arise because public opinion in the area has been inflamed either by the nature of the crime or by publicity in the media. Courts seek to prevent material appearing in the media that could have a damaging effect, and they have punitive powers. However, it is not only comments in the media about the particular crime but also general comments upon that class of crime that can inflame a jury's mind.

Criticisms of juries in civil cases

The criticisms expressed above in relation to exemptions from jury service and ineligibility to serve on a jury in criminal cases also apply to civil juries. So also do the criticisms relating to unfamiliarity with court procedure, lack of experience in considering arguments over a lengthy period, and lack of transcript and note-taking facilities.

By the very nature of the jury, those composing the jury are not likely to be familiar with current awards of damages except for those which have obtained headlines in the media. Such knowledge that they have of awards of damages, therefore, is likely to be knowledge of the higher amounts. This knowledge, which may fairly be described as inflationary in its effect, is knowledge given by the media to persons who have no training in the assessment of damages.

Extension or restriction of the use of juries in criminal cases

A fact often lost sight of is that most criminal cases are heard, not by a judge and jury, but in a magistrates' court. That fact is, however, not a reflection upon the jury system but is an exemplification of the tremendous growth in statutory offences, most of which are offences which by Act of Parliament have to be heard in a magistrates' court. Parliament itself, when creating new offences, tends to require them to be heard in a magistrates' court rather than by judge and jury.

Extending the jury system to magistrates' courts would be impracticable. In the first place, it would require the attendance of a very large number of prospective jurors because of the large number of cases that come before the magistrates' courts. Introducing the jury into the magistrates' court system would lead to great delays in a system that is already overloaded. Another important factor is that magistrates lack the experience, training and authority of a judge, and their rulings would therefore carry less weight with the jury: their whole training is not designed to fulfil that function.

Regard also has to be had to the nature of cases coming before magistrates' courts. Is it really necessary to have 13 people (a magistrate and a jury of twelve) to decide whether or not a motorist has exceeded – as so many do – the speed limit on a motorway? The nature of the offence, and the comparatively small amount of the penalty, do not justify what would be using a sledgehammer to crack a nut. There are, however, some cases which presently come for trial in a magistrates' court which could more properly be brought before a judge and jury: there is a need to reassess where the line should be drawn and to ensure that all cases of sufficient importance go to a jury and that only cases of that importance do so.

There is an argument for substituting trial by judge for trial by jury in those cases in which community prejudices have been aroused either by the nature of the alleged crime or by the media. Those cases are exceptional, but they do exist. It might be very much to the advantage of the accused in such a case to be able to apply for trial by a judge without a jury. Trial by jury may also be thought to be outmoded in some of the more complex cases that modern society produces. For example, some of the more complex 'white collar' frauds may involve accounting and other issues that are beyond the expertise of the criminal jury and that really need trial by a judge without a jury. Alternatively, for the concept of a jury drawn generally from the community as a whole (subject, however, under the present system to substantial exemptions and categories of ineligibility) there could be substituted the concept of a jury of a specialised nature for such a specialised case. If it is said that a specialised jury of that nature alters the concept of the jury system, at least it can be said that it would be trial by peers.

Jury reforms

The most obvious area for reform of the jury system lies in a wider eligibility for jury service. There is much to be said for limiting the right to challenge to a right to challenge only when good cause for that challenge can be shown. However, the value of this reform, in giving a better cross-section of the community on the jury, has to be weighed against the importance of allowing the accused to play an effective part in the selection of the tribunal by which the accused will be tried.

A preparatory explanation of court procedure to the prospective jurors before they come into the courtroom, and an opportunity at that stage to ask questions about that procedure, would be of advantage to them. So also would be the provision of note-taking facilities. Provision of a transcript is perhaps more questionable, for it might be more confusing than advantageous: a transcript records everything said in court, and makes dull and lengthy reading. It is often hard to find some particular statement in the transcript because there is no index to it. The transcript would have to be edited for a jury because there are questions of law which, in fairness to the accused, are argued before the judge in the absence of the jury.

CHAPTER 17

THE PUNISHMENT OF OFFENDERS

The principal purposes of the criminal law

It is against the principal purposes of the criminal law that the various means of punishment of offenders must be weighed. The best known purposes of the criminal law are punishment, deterrence and reform. Popular argument on the matter is often confined to these purposes, but a more detailed analysis will reveal many more, as can be seen from the following list:

(a) Preserve the fundamental basis of the society in which it is administered.

(b) Preserve public order.

(c) Render it unnecessary for persons to take the law into their own hands.

(d) Prevent conduct offensive to the prevailing sense of public decency.

(e) Prevent conduct currently regarded as blasphemous.

(f) Protect property and other rights.

(g) Prevent abuses in public administration and in the exercise of police powers.

(h) Protect public health.

(i) Protect members of the public in circumstances in which they could not protect themselves.

(j) Preserve the environment.

(k) Punish, reform and deter.

Any society can be expected to attempt to preserve its own fundamental beliefs. What those beliefs are may vary widely, from the medieval church's belief in its own status and the purity of its doctrine as exemplified in its canon law to the communist state's requirement of 'socialist justice' as overriding the citizen's legal rights, to modern western society's emphasis on the rights of the individual as being fundamental. This last aspect can best be seen in the Constitution of the United States of America. No society can be expected to accept its own violent overthrow. This does not mean that the protection given by the law to its fundamental attitudes and beliefs prevents all change: as attitudes change the law may be changed also. The criminal law is employed to protect the fundamental attitudes of a society as they exist at a particular time.

It is a purpose of the criminal law to preserve public order. Crimes against public order are well known. It is a crime to assault the police, or to interfere with a police officer in the exercise of his or her duties. Riot is a crime, and so also is inciting a riot. The support given by the law to public order is common to almost all societies. It is the nature of that protection, and how far it is to be balanced against other considerations such as the right to protest, which causes the difficulty.

An important purpose of the criminal law in modern society is to render it unnecessary for people to take the law into their own hands. In a primitive society personal enforcement of the criminal law by the person injured by its breach is one of the norms of society. Today, there are certain circumstances in which private individuals can take the enforcement of the criminal law into their own hands, but only within the judicial system of the courts: unless the right is excluded by statute, any member of the community can prosecute for a breach of the criminal law, but that community member prosecutes not by dealing personally with the alleged offender but by bringing the alleged offender before the courts. The attitude of the law to people who take the enforcement of the criminal law into their own hands has changed markedly in recent centuries. There was a time when it was lawful for a man to protect his property against poachers by mantraps and spring guns. A mantrap was a steel trap, like an animal trap, with a strong spring, capable of holding a man prisoner as well as inflicting painful injuries upon him. Since he would be incapable of freeing himself, if not released he might well die in the trap. Spring guns were loaded weapons set to fire when a tripwire was touched. The poacher who touched such a wire might well be killed. Nowadays any person who used such devices would be prosecuted for murder if the trespasser died. In Ireland some centuries ago a man of 70 was knighted for killing four burglars with a carving knife; nowadays, even if physically attacked, anyone who uses too much force in self-defence will be tried as a criminal.

Another purpose of the criminal law is to prevent conduct offensive to the prevailing sense of public decency. What will offend against public decency will, of course, vary from society to society and from age to age. Morality in the 19th century required swimmers to be completely covered from neck to ankle, but the bikini is commonplace today.

Conduct regarded as blasphemous is prohibited by the criminal law in all societies from the primitive to the modern. Like questions of public decency, questions of blasphemy are ones in respect of which there will be considerable changes from society to society and from age to age. In modern times conduct blasphemous in the strict religious sense is no longer regarded by the law as seriously as it was. However, offences such as racial discrimination are viewed by many people as morally offensive in much the same way; and in Britain legislation has been passed to outlaw such conduct. In most societies from the primitive to the modern it is a purpose of the criminal law to protect property and other rights. For example, theft is a crime and so it ought to be.

In a primitive society there is no public administration and no organised police force such as exists in a modern State. Even in medieval England, however, although there was no organised large-scale police force, there was a form of public (royal) administration; and abuses in it led to repeated troubles such as produced Magna Carta. As bureaucracy increases, the need to prevent abuses in public administration becomes more widespread.

The protection of public health is a purpose of the criminal law which has developed as such particularly within the last century and a half. However, laws controlling building, and making it a criminal offence not to comply with them, go back in the City of London to immediately after the Great Fire of London in 1666. Typical public health laws today, in addition to such matters as building control, are laws requiring cleanliness in shops in which food is sold and vehicles in which food is carried, and laws regulating the purity and standards of food. Some of those standards have been the subject of directives issued by the European Community.

It is a purpose of the criminal law to protect members of the public in circumstances in which they could not protect themselves. The criminal offences created by modern consumer protection legislation afford a recent example.[1] The preservation of the environment falls within the purposes of the criminal law, although much of its development has been recent. The environment is a matter that has elicited growing attention from Parliament. On 19 July 1995 the latest statute in this field received the Royal Assent. It consists of 125 sections and 24 schedules.[2]

This analysis of the principal purposes of the criminal law must not cause the reader to lose sight of the fact that fundamental purposes of the criminal law are to punish offenders, reform offenders, and deter persons from offending. How those fundamental purposes are to be fulfilled is something upon which opinions differ considerably.

The purposes of punishment

There are various theories underlying the imposition of a penalty. It may be imposed for its reformative effect, or as a deterrent to the offender against offending again, or to the community generally against committing that offence, or as a preventive measure to stop the offender committing offences again over a period, or for punitive purposes. Punishment also serves a further purpose in that each time an offender is punished, society reaffirms the values which the offender's conduct has challenged. In some cases the challenge to accepted values is tacit, and is a mere side effect of the conduct itself, in other cases a deliberate challenge is made to society's accepted values. Very often such a challenge is made by a minority, which may be small but very vocal. The conviction of this type of offender by ordinary members of the community sitting on a jury reaffirms to the rest of society that the values under challenge are still supported by most people. Failure to reaffirm the values of society consistently in such a way can lead to the weakening of the values themselves.

The punitive purpose was probably the original purpose of penalties. Penalties intended as deterrents can be seen in the tendency of the courts to impose much heavier sentences when a particular crime becomes prevalent. Preventive penalties are those imposed by way of long-term imprisonment; they have their effect because the offender cannot offend again while in prison if the prison system is properly conducted. Another preventive measure used is imprisonment of indefinite length, a system usually used in the case of habitual offenders.

The reformative aspect of penalty is a mark of a society which cares for the individual, and its importance as a theory regulating the imposition of penalties has increased very considerably in recent times both in relation to the methods used and in relation to the frequency of its use. Homes for juveniles are intended to achieve reformation. They may also be used for the purpose of

---

1   See, for example, the Restrictive Trade Practices Act 1976 and the Restrictive Trade Practices Act 1977.

2   Environment Act 1995.

removing the juvenile from circumstances of moral danger such as association with undesirables. Their effectiveness in the latter regard, however, must be limited by the very nature of the inmates in the juvenile home itself. Unfortunately the reform of criminals is extremely difficult and the results in individual cases are hard to predict. The problem is that the criminal must want to change an entire lifestyle and way of thinking. As with dieting, promises are easy to make but relapses are all too common.

Capital punishment

The death penalty is a punishment which was at one time imposed very extensively. It reached its maximum usage in the early 19th century. Since then its use has been declining, and in most modern western societies it is now either very rare or else has been abolished. Views upon capital punishment vary considerably in the community. This is exemplified by the return to capital punishment in various States of the USA.

Dislike of capital punishment, and doubts about its effectiveness, are almost confined to modern western societies. In Islamic societies, for example, the death penalty (along with other punishments commonly regarded as barbarous) is quite frequently employed. The difference is partly one of philosophy and religion, but may also be due to the higher living standards in the West and the consequent greater value placed on human life.

Capital punishment, if carried out, cannot be reformative of the particular criminal; but to what extent is the threat of it a deterrent? What is a distant prospect may have neither a strong deterrent nor a powerful reformative effect, for many people hope that they may not be caught. However, a case is known of the imminent threat of capital punishment having a reformative effect. The case is one in which the accused was a man who had abandoned his trade and who was living in a boarding house of poor standard. He fired a rifle through the door of a room in which he knew there was a person with whom he had quarrelled. The trial lasted several days and was at a time when capital punishment was still on the statute books and when there was a risk of it being carried out. He was acquitted. As he said years afterwards, the threat of the rope made such an impression upon him that he returned to his former trade, worked his way up to foreman, married, and settled down with his family.

Imprisonment

What constitutes imprisonment is of course well known. It is perhaps not so well known that there are different kinds of prisons. The severity of the punishment in a maximum security division of a prison is very much greater than that on an open prison farm. In both cases the prisoner is deprived of liberty; but in the case of the maximum security prison the prisoner is also much more limited in terms of social contact, exercise and fresh air, and variety in life. The maximum security prisoner is restrained by iron bars and spends much time in a cell; the prisoner in an open prison who wishes to escape, has only to walk off the farm and evade pursuit. Of course, the prisoner who does escape and is later caught will be sent to a much harsher regime as well as being punished for the escape. The effects of the different types of imprisonment may vary quite widely, both on the prisoner and on the family. It is difficult to determine how far either sort of imprisonment is effective as a deterrent.

There are statistics to show the prison population at various times, the numbers of prisoners by sex and by age, the length of terms of imprisonment being served, and the number of recidivists (that is, the number serving a second or subsequent prison term). There cannot, however, be any statistics to show how many additional prisoners there would have been if any of the various forms of penalties consequent upon the infringement of the criminal law did not exist. It is known that various people would offend against the criminal law in any event: the very harsh penalties imposed for breaches of the criminal law in England in the late 18th and early 19th centuries, and the very harsh penalties imposed in Russia, do not create a society that is free from crime: even a totalitarian State cannot achieve that.

The difficulties inherent in such statistics as are available, and the problems of using those statistics, are highlighted by a report published by the National Association for the Care and Resettlement of Offenders. The report, by the Exeter Community Policing Consultative Group, states that:

> It is hard to measure the success of preventive measures ... Statistics as a measurement of success are more likely to be misleading than clarifying, except possibly over a long period of time. For example, crime figures may rise as a community becomes more self-confident, not because people report more to the police.

The effectiveness of prison as a punishment is hampered by a conflict between priorities. If deterrence is what is wanted, the harsh regime of a maximum security prison is likely to have the greatest effect. Such a regime, however, is likely to leave the criminal at the end of the term of imprisonment unfit to re-enter society both because of being unused to freedom and because some, perhaps many, may have no trade. Reformation is best assisted by an open prison regime where the prisoner is trusted with limited freedom and has opportunities to learn a trade; yet, if the punishment is seen as too lenient, its deterrent effect may disappear.

Psychiatric treatment during imprisonment

An offender who is actually insane at the time of committing the offence cannot properly be convicted as a criminal; but, as the finding of insanity is a jury function, error is possible in a field unknown to most, if not all, the jurors. Insanity is a defence to a criminal charge, but a person found not guilty on grounds of insanity is not simply released. Release on grounds of insanity would cause a community outcry since it would leave the insane one free to commit the same offence, and again with free discharge into the community. What actually happens is that the person who commits a crime whilst insane is confined to a hospital for the criminally insane where treatment will be administered, and (subject to the possibility of a short release or releases on a test basis) release will not be granted until such time, if at all, as the doctors there believe a cure has been effected. This may mean a longer term of imprisonment than would be the case for a sane criminal who committed the same offence.

A problem arises if the convicted criminal does not consent to the use of the particular treatment. Imprisonment involves deprivation of liberty; psychiatric treatment involves changing a person's mind and character. To change a person's whole personality without the consent or against the wishes of that person is not only very difficult, it is a far worse invasion of liberty than mere imprisonment could ever be. It has been notorious that in Russia this very procedure has been used against people whose only crime was to disagree with the State, and it has been used to brand them as mad and to subject them to harmful drugs and electric shock treatments. This kind of treatment is thought by some to have a useful effect on the insane, but to impose it without a person's own consent is plainly torture. The alternative from the community viewpoint may well be imprisonment until consent or death; yet imprisonment upon that basis is subject to a right of appeal against its severity, and an appellate court would be unlikely to uphold such a sentence.

Work release

The work release system is used in respect of prisoners who are nearing the end of their term of imprisonment. They are allowed to work in ordinary jobs in the community during the day but are required to return to prison each evening.

Periodic detention

One of the great disadvantages of a prison sentence is that it takes the offender out of the community, sometimes for a long period, and it may have the effect that the offender finds upon release an unfitness for life in the community. Periodic detention enables a convicted criminal to serve the term of imprisonment during leisure time. The offender is not deprived of a job, and is able both to spend time with the family and to support them financially. However, the convicted person is reminded, over a period, of the community's disapproval of the offence by having to attend repeatedly at a centre during the evening or during a weekend. Periodic deprival of leisure time, combined with a greater involvement in the life of the local community, may be of very great assistance in the reform of an offender. Care is exercised in choosing those who are to attend such a programme, with the aim of selecting those who are likely to be reformed. Such a programme is not likely to succeed if the offender is unwilling to co-operate; but, with co-operation, it gives a much better chance than prison could of being wholly reformed and reintegrated into the life of the community.

Work orders

A possible sanction that is worth considering in cases of damage to public property, cases such as vandalism, is that of requiring the offender not only to make good the damage but to protect that property or similar property over a specified period of time. Such a system might inculcate in the offender a sense of responsibility for property of that type or at least a dislike for that type of anti-social behaviour.

Youth training centres

In earlier times no distinction was made between the young criminal and the hardened criminal. Both were placed in the same prison. This brought the young offender into contact with hardened criminals, with the risk of the young offender gaining an education in crime through the term of imprisonment. The modern concept is that of youth training centres in which the young offender is kept in an institution to which the older criminals are not admitted. The young offender may still be in contact with hardened criminals, for some of the young offenders may themselves fall into that category; but at least there is not the influence of the older and therefore more experienced criminals. As their name indicates, youth training centres have a strong emphasis upon training, with the intent that the young offender, upon release, will have a trade to pursue.

Corporal punishment

Corporal punishment is often attacked in western societies as contrary to human rights. However, some criminals may be sufficiently shocked by corporal punishment to be deterred from committing further offences of that nature. One suggestion that was put forward but has not been acted upon is in relation to corporal punishment for crimes of rape or of armed crime. What was advocated is administering a caning on entrance to prison, upon each anniversary of the crime, and on the day of leaving prison.

In a book written by Morris QC[3] he tells the story of a South African magistrate who sentenced black women shoplifters to a caning with the result that shoplifting in that town ceased overnight. In Fiji, the experience is that persons sentenced to imprisonment and a caning in the lower court would appeal to the Supreme Court for the prison sentence to be lengthened and to be relieved of the caning. Do these examples indicate that corporal punishment is an effective deterrent? Again, there is the problem of the unreliability of statistics. Both instances, it should be noted, are of persons from the less affluent sectors of society, and it may be that in both cases it is the humiliation which has the real effect. The importance of these examples lies in the emphasis of the difficulties of using statistics relating to crime and to the measures to combat crime.

Fine

The effect of any financial penalty depends in part on the wealth and income of the offender. A fine which would be a severe punishment to a poor person may have little effect on a rich one. The penalties in fact imposed tend to be inflicted without regard to the offender's income (which is not, in any case, proved by evidence before the court). However, a fine which is not a severe financial penalty may yet have a deterrent effect. It is often the case that an offender has a strong dislike of being convicted as a criminal, no matter how light the penalty

---

3 *My First Forty Years.*

may be. This fact is used by officers to persuade offenders against health controls to spend money in preventing future offences, on the basis that a prosecution would thereafter be dropped.

Suspended sentence

The suspended system operates by proceeding not only to the point of conviction but to the imposition of the appropriate sentence for the offence. The accused is not only found guilty of the offence but is told what, in the court's opinion, is the appropriate sentence to be served if that sentence were not being suspended. The sentence is then suspended to give an opportunity to prove that the offender can thereafter act as a responsible law-abiding member of the community without the need for the punishment of imprisonment. Sentence is usually suspended for a substantial period during which the offender has the threat of that sentence of imprisonment hanging over him or her; for, if the offender offends again during that period, the suspended sentence immediately takes effect as a sentence of imprisonment. The question as to whether a suspended sentence is the appropriate sentence from the community viewpoint, as distinct from the viewpoint of rehabilitating the individual offender, has its problems.

Bond

The system of releasing an offender upon a bond involves substituting the threat of punishment for actual punishment. Such an offender is required to enter into an undertaking to be of good behaviour. This undertaking is given in writing, and is subject to a condition that, if there is failure to comply with that undertaking, the offender will forfeit a sum of money specified in the bond. Upon breach of the bond the offender is not only dealt with for the new offence and the breach itself, but also forfeits that sum of money to the Crown.

Bonds are frequently used in the case of first offenders. They can, however, be used with success even in the case of offenders with repeated convictions. It is an interesting fact appearing from statistics relating to offenders that recidivism (that is, repeated committing of offences) occurs less frequently in the case of prisoners in their later forties and older.

Adjournment

A court, instead of convicting an offender, may decide to adjourn the hearing at the stage at which guilt has been established. In this way it gives the offender a specified period, often a period of 12 months, in which to prove that he or she does not intend to offend again; and, if that period is completed successfully, there is a discharge without the stain of a conviction.

Another method by which adjournment is used is that of adjourning prior to the commencement of the hearing of the case. This use of the adjournment power is a means of overcoming inadequate penalties imposed by Parliament or by subordinate legislation. For example, there may be a need to persuade the offender to clean up his or her premises or to adopt other health or environmental measures. The offender may be anxious to avoid the stigma of a conviction, and an adjournment without conviction subject to compliance with the requirements of the law may be more effective from the community viewpoint than proceeding to a conviction and a small fine.

Parole

Another method employed is that of the parole system. Under this system a person who has been sentenced to imprisonment may be released before the completion of the prescribed term of imprisonment and subject to good behaviour and subject to any directions that may be given to the offender by an officer appointed for that purpose. The offender who breaks parole by committing a further offence, or by failing to comply with any directions, can be reimprisoned to complete the unexpired portion of the prison sentence (and, of course, can also be punished for the further offence).

Probation

Probation is essentially very similar to parole, but it is imposed as an alternative to imprisonment instead of on early release from a prison sentence. The offender is required to report regularly to the probation officer, and is subject to that officer's control.

The punishment of juvenile offenders

It is a mark of modern society that it treats the juvenile offender differently from the offender beyond juvenile years. Except for major crimes such as murder, the juvenile offender is dealt with by a special court. Whereas offenders are normally dealt with in open court with the press and the public having a right of admission, juvenile offenders are dealt with in private: those present are limited to the magistrate, the magistrate's clerk, the prosecutor, the witnesses, the juvenile accused, and the parents of the accused (together, of course, with the legal representatives, if any, for the accused).

The difficulty of sentencing

Individuals within the community vary very widely not only in their attitude to law but also in their reaction to punishment. There is no simple system by which a judge can say that a person who had committed a particular offence (or who has a history of committing particular offences) will react in a standard way to a standard punishment. The judge, when sentencing, may have assistance from psychiatrists, the reports of police and probation officers, witnesses to character, and the judge's own opinion formed during the trial about the offender's character and willingness to reform. It remains an exceedingly difficult task to choose among the many varieties of punishment available that one which will be most appropriate to the particular offender in the circumstances of the particular case.

The changing approach to punishment

Over the last few centuries there have been very great changes in the economy, the government, and most other aspects of western societies. It would be surprising if our attitude to punishment had not changed as well. In the society of the 18th and early 19th century when property was regarded more highly as a fundamental social value than it is today, and when human life counted for less, punishments were freely used which today might be regarded as unconscionable – notably capital punishment and corporal punishment.

The Constitution of the United States of America contains a prohibition of 'cruel and unusual' punishments. Whether a provision is regarded as cruel must depend very largely upon the views of society, and whether it is unusual must also depend to a large extent on how much it is used in practice.

The general public's desire for imprisonment, or for long terms of imprisonment, for offenders appears to vary from time to time. The evaluation of the effectiveness of imprisonment and of the various alternative punishments is difficult even for those expert in the field.

CHAPTER 18

THE INEVITABILITY OF LIMITATIONS

Human frailties within the legal system

No legal system can be devised to exclude the human element totally. Whether the system exists under a dictatorship or a democracy, there must be individual judges and individuals enforcing the law. In 19th century Prussia, Frederick the Great attempted to lay down a complete system of rules and to exclude interpretation by the judges. The aim was to prescribe a rule to meet every situation. In practice, of course, situations continually arose which the rules laid down did not cover. Modern codes, therefore, tend to be laid down on much broader lines, and to leave considerable scope for the judges to interpret them (and, in practice, codes represent only a small part of our rules of law).

The individual member of the police force or customs officer or departmental inspector is not, and never can be, a mere robot sent out to enforce the law. There are so many legal rules which it is their duty to enforce that it is impossible for them to check up on everybody all the time – and the community would strongly object if an attempt were made to do so. It is necessary for the law enforcement officers, even at the lowest level, to have a large measure of discretion as to the rules they concentrate on enforcing, and as to the way in which they go about doing so. The member of the police force who detects someone committing a motoring offence must make the decision whether to prosecute or to warn, or even to ignore it in the interests of preventing some more serious crime. Superior officers will lay down broad priorities, but they cannot lay down rules to cover every detailed situation. Personal experience, and colleagues' advice, are factors upon which law enforcement officers must rely – and also any statements of government policy.

An individual law enforcement officer, enforcing a particular section of an Act or a particular statutory instrument, may find that it has never been interpreted by the judges. Enforcement of that law cannot be suspended until such time as some case has come before the judges for it to be interpreted. Indeed, in the ordinary way, such a case would only come before the judges if a law enforcement officer had attempted to enforce that law: it is by the process of prosecution and appeal that such questions of interpretation do come before the judges. In our system of law the courts are not there to answer hypothetical questions, and they have shown themselves to be reluctant in proceedings other than a prosecution to express views on whether or not particular conduct constitutes a criminal offence – adopting the attitude that that is a matter to be decided in the ordinary administration of the criminal law. In the leading case, in which the House of Lords reversed the English Court of Appeal's decision and refused to grant a declaration as to whether or not particular conduct constituted a breach of the criminal law, Viscount Dilhorne said:

> Could the court in the proper exercise of its discretion grant the declaration sought? Donaldson J [the judge before whom the case first came and later Lord Donaldson of Lymington MR] thought it could but did not grant it as he thought that the ... scheme was a lottery and an unlawful competition. The Court of Appeal, holding that it was neither, granted it.

That decision, if it stands, will form a precedent for the Commercial Court and other civil courts usurping the functions of the criminal courts. Publishers may be tempted to seek declarations that what they propose to publish is not a criminal libel or blasphemous or obscene. If in this case, where the declaration sought was not in respect of future conduct but in respect of what had already taken place, it could properly be granted, I see no reason why in such cases a declaration as to future conduct could not be granted. If this were to happen, then the position would be much the same as it was before the passing of Fox's Libel Act 1792 [England] when judges, not juries, decided whether a libel was criminal, blasphemous or obscene.

Such a declaration is no bar to a criminal prosecution, no matter the authority of the court which grants it. Such a declaration in a case such as the present one, made after the commencement of the prosecution, and in effect a finding of guilt or innocence of the offence charged, cannot found a plea of *autrefois* acquit or *autrefois* convict, though it may well prejudice the criminal proceedings, the result of which will depend on the facts proved and may not depend solely on admissions made by the accused. If a civil court of great authority declares on admissions made by the accused that no crime has been committed, one can foresee the use that might be made of that at the criminal trial.

The justification for the Court of Appeal taking this unusual and unprecedented course – no case was cited to us where a civil court had, after the commencement of a prosecution, granted a declaration that no offence had been committed – was said to be the length of time it would have taken for the matter to be determined in the criminal courts. I can well see the advantages of persons being able to obtain rulings on whether or not certain conduct on which they propose to embark will be criminal and it may be a defect in our present system that it does not provide for that. Here, I wish to emphasise, it was not a question whether future conduct would be permissible but whether acts done were criminal. It was said that the administration of justice would belie its name if civil courts refused to answer reasonable questions on whether certain conduct was or was not lawful. I do not agree. I think that the administration of justice would become chaotic if after the start of a prosecution, declarations of innocence could be obtained from a civil court.

What was the urgency in the present case? The operation of the scheme began in October 1978. It was to end on 31 March 1979. It may be that far too much time elapses nowadays before accused persons are tried on indictment but why should these respondents be singled out for special treatment? I do not see that there was any particular urgency or that there was any special reason for the respondents to be treated differently from other accused. If the case had been tried summarily in the magistrates' court at Nottingham, I doubt if it would have taken longer, or an appreciable time longer to reach this House. All the cases on lotteries to which I have referred were, with one exception, tried in the magistrates' courts. The exception is *R v Harris*[1] where the trial was on indictment. In my opinion a magistrates' court is the best court for the determination of the question, where there is a genuine dispute, as to whether or not a scheme is an unlawful lottery or unlawful competition, for whatever the result, there can be an appeal by way of case stated on facts found by the magistrates. There can, of course, be no appeal should a trial on indictment result in a verdict of not guilty. In this case the director said that he would seek trial on indictment, presumably because it was felt that the magistrates would not have

---

1   10 Cox CC 352.

power to impose a heavy enough penalty. Whether in a case such as this when the respondents honestly believed in the light of the legal advice they had received that the scheme was lawful, a Crown Court would have imposed a heavier penalty than the magistrates may be open to doubt.

My Lords, it is not necessary in this case to decide whether a declaration as to the criminality or otherwise of future conduct can ever properly be made by a civil court. In my opinion it would be a very exceptional case in which it would be right to do so. In my opinion it cannot be right to grant a declaration that an accused is innocent after a prosecution has started.[2]

In the same case Lord Lane said that

There is no doubt that there is jurisdiction to grant a declaration in these circumstances. Anyone is on principle entitled to apply to the court for a declaration as to their rights unless statutorily prohibited expressly or by necessary implication ... There was no such prohibition here; but was the learned judge right to exercise his discretion as he did, as the Court of Appeal thought he was? ...

It would be strange if a defendant to proper criminal proceedings were able to pre-empt those proceedings by application to a judge of the High Court whether sitting in the Commercial Court or elsewhere. What effect in law upon the criminal proceedings would any pronouncement from the High Court in these circumstances have? The criminal court would not be bound by the decision. In practical terms it would simply have the inevitable effect of prejudicing the criminal trial one way or the other.

Where there are concurrent proceedings in different courts between parties who for practical purposes are the same in each, and the same issue will have to be determined in each, the court has jurisdiction to stay one set of proceedings if it is just and convenient to do so or if the circumstances are such that one set of proceedings is vexatious and an abuse of the process of the court. Where, however, criminal proceedings have been properly instituted and are not vexatious or an abuse of the process of the court, it is not a proper exercise of the court's discretion to grant to the defendant in those proceedings a declaration that the facts to be alleged by the prosecution do not in law prove the offence charged.[3]

To illustrate the human frailties within the system it is worth pointing out that, although Viscount Dilhorne said that 'no case was cited to us where a civil court had after the commencement of a prosecution, granted a declaration that no offence had been committed', such a declaration had been granted by the High Court of Australia two years previously (in what it regarded as an exceptional case).[4]

Judges themselves are human beings and subject to human frailties. It is of course true that every judge will try to achieve a just result within the framework of existing law, but the ability to do so is limited by expertise or lack of it in the particular field, by the judge's ability and by the existing state of the law. Some judges are more conservative than others, and some are readier to expand the existing legal principles. The very fact that a case reaches the

---

2   *Imperial Tobacco Ltd v Attorney General* [1981] AC 718, Viscount Dilhorne at 741–42.

3   *Imperial Tobacco Ltd v Attorney General* [1981] AC 718, Lord Lane at 750 and 752.

4   *Sankey v Whitlam* (1978) 142 CLR 1.

superior courts normally means that there are arguments to be put on both sides. When it is possible for a judge to decide the case by taking the view of the law argued for by one side or the different view contended for by the other side without violating the basic principles of the existing law, the attitude of the individual judge is necessarily of great importance. The experienced lawyer may therefore adapt the presentation of a case to accord with the particular type of court in which the presentation of the case is being made and to accord with the approach that the particular judge or magistrate prefers to adopt. This is an aspect of the legal system that no 'reform' could obviate.

Our present legal system is designed to give every assistance to the judge's efforts to achieve an impartial and just result through the use of the adversary system. Where, as in Europe, the system is inquisitorial, the judge must personally examine witnesses; and judicial predilections play a greater role. Under the adversary system of law the judge hears first one side and then the other, and it is up to the lawyers concerned to test each other's arguments and witnesses. The judge is not personally concerned with attacking particular witnesses, but with assessing them. The adversary system therefore limits human frailties, but it cannot obviate them; and it is subject to the limitation that the barristers themselves are inevitably of differing calibre and experience.

In assessing the limitations which human frailties impose upon any legal system it is important to remember that justice is not a coin-in-the-slot machine and that any attempt to reduce it to such a concept would not be a furtherance, but a denial, of justice.

Conflicting needs of perfection, certainty and speed

Perfect justice would provide the ideal solution to every particular case. This would tend to involve the consideration of every case at the highest level, but even at the highest level judges can be in disagreement. This is particularly so in relation to the proper interpretation of legislation. There are numerous cases in the House of Lords where five judges of the highest experience and reputation have been of divided views, three deciding one way and two another. There have also been cases in which even the House of Lords has, with reluctance, overruled its own previous decisions. Perfection is therefore unattainable, and even the pursuit of perfection can lead to difficulties. In many cases what is required is not a perfect answer but a swift, certain and acceptable one. Justice delayed is justice denied, and the judge who takes too long in trying to reach the perfect judgment may in fact deny justice to the particular litigants whose case is awaiting decision (for example, the litigant may have died or circumstances may have so altered that the successful litigant is unable to make use of that success).

Certainty in the law is of very great importance. A large proportion of cases in which a writ is issued never comes before the courts because the cases are settled – that is, the parties come to a voluntary agreement, aided in doing so by the fact that their lawyers are able to assess what the result is likely to be. In the absence of certainty, if the courts swung widely between one result and the other or as to the amount of damages imposed, it would be much more difficult to achieve settlements and the courts would be even more overloaded by litigation. This would make it much more difficult for the courts to devote sufficient time to each case. It would also produce problems within the community itself, for commercial decisions have to be made within the framework of the legal system: the industrialist who enters into a contract to supply goods, and the department store that sends its buyers across the world, must be able to rely upon the approach of the legal system in the interpretation of those contracts. Complete certainty, however, is unattainable. The inevitable lack of complete certainty in any legal system arises from a number of factors – the frailties of human recollection leading to differing versions of what has occurred, the inevitability of different interpretations of the words that have been used, and the changing approaches of courts and of individual judges as community conditions and values change.

Delays in obtaining a decision before the courts probably cause more complaint than any other aspect of our legal system. Those who are involved in litigation are left in a state of suspense and anxiety, sometimes for years, and may be unable to formulate firm plans for their future during that time because of the possible heavy financial commitment which a court decision may or may not impose upon them. There are rare circumstances when it is important not to bring a case on for hearing too fast – as, for instance, where damage has been suffered but it is not yet certain just how serious that damage is going to be (a person who suffers damage to a joint in an accident may not be able to find out for years whether or not this will lead to osteoarthritis). In most cases, however, a delayed decision does not advantage either the litigants or the community. The ideals of perfection and certainty are inevitably in conflict with the need for speedy justice.

The importance of knowing the limitations of the legal system

It is important not to allow regard for a 'system' to obscure the reality. Overreliance upon a system can lead to social disaster if that system fails to achieve what the community has been led to expect of it. No system is perfect, and an expectation of perfection must result in disappointment. Disappointment engendered in that way can lead to demands for change that, because of failure to appreciate the imperfections and the causes of the imperfections in the system, not only may lead to no real improvement but may even aggravate what they are intended to cure. It is important, therefore, to bear in mind that our legal system does have its imperfections. It is equally important, however, to bear in mind that our legal system, with all its imperfections, has given us and preserved for us a stable society that (within its own limitations) is able to cope even with rapidly changing conditions.

CHAPTER 19

LIMITATIONS ON THE EFFECTIVENESS OF PARLIAMENT

The purpose of Parliament

Parliament is the body which makes statute law, also referred to as legislation or as Acts of Parliament. Today this is its best-known function, but Parliament has always had another purpose. This purpose is to represent the interests of the people as against the government, to express the grievances of the people and to press for reform. In medieval times Parliament's main function was to deal with grievances and to authorise taxation: the idea that the law could be changed in any fundamental way by Parliament arose only more recently. For most of its history Parliament was separate from the executive – and often found itself in opposition to it (a situation which still exists in the United States of America today). Ironically, it is the very victory of Parliament over the executive and the resulting necessity for members of the government to be drawn from the leading party, or parties, in Parliament which has changed that situation: the very victory of Parliament has tended to reduce its importance. Except for the occasional 'back bench revolt' Parliament now plays a supporting role behind the Cabinet, which is, of course, at the head of the Executive.

The changes in the role of Parliament have not affected its power to make new law, but they have affected the purposes for which that power is likely to be used. Instead of redressing the grievances of the people those powers are now largely used to carry out the policy of the government. One symptom of that change is the decline in the importance of the private member's Bill to the point where it has become a rarity.

Limitations on the choice of members of the House of Commons

There was a time when the membership of Parliament was limited, partly because members were unpaid and therefore had to have private financial resources, and partly due to a property qualification for election to the House of Commons. At that time there were seats which were actually in the gift of a particular person, either through traditional loyalty to him and his family or because he was able to bribe the very few people who had the right to vote. These were known as 'pocket boroughs' and 'rotten boroughs'. The most notorious example is of a manor which had had the right to send a member to Parliament – the sea had encroached and completely covered the manor, but the lord of that manor still had the right to send a member to Parliament even although no one lived where the land had formerly been!

The abolition of pocket and rotten boroughs and the extension of the right to vote for members of the House of Commons to all adults ended this kind of limitation on the choice of persons available for election to Parliament. Payment of members has also widened the choice, since almost anyone can now afford to stand as a candidate for Parliament, although there are people who would suffer a reduction in their income if they were elected.

Membership of the House of Lords has not been affected to the same extent. From time to time one or more politicians may be elevated to the House of Lords as a life peer – that is, as one whose peerage ends on that peer's death instead of being inherited. There are certain offices that necessarily require the officeholder to be an existing member of the House of Lords or to be elevated to the peerage on appointment to an office in that category: the distinguished office of Lord Chancellor is an example.

As the old limitations were destroyed, new ones have sprung up. The growth and increasing rigidity of the party system has limited the effective choice in most cases to the House of Commons candidates put up by the parties. Independent candidates do stand, and occasionally one is elected. Indeed, the power of the party system is so great in the hands of the major parties that it has become very difficult for a new party (as opposed to an old party reorganised under a new name) to become a major force in Parliament. In many cases more candidates are eliminated in the party selection committees than are eliminated at the polls.

In a 'safe seat', always held by the same party, the public effectively has no say at all in who is to be the member of Parliament. The party which holds that safe seat selects its candidate, probably from among numerous contenders; but it is the party members or party executive and not the public who make the selection. By the very nature of its being a 'safe seat' any other candidates who stand have little chance of being elected. It is perfectly possible in such a case for a candidate to be selected not on the ground of any likely contribution to Parliament but on the ground of service to the party machine.

Limitations on representation of sections of the community

The system under which members of Parliament are elected to the Commons, is a system by which only one person represents any particular electorate. No matter how closely a particular election may be contested, one person and one person only represents that electorate. There have been several instances in the post-war years of seats won by a handful of votes. When a seat is won so narrowly, nearly half the voters in that electorate are holding views opposed to the political views of the person representing that electorate. Their political views cannot be expressed in Parliament through their local member. It is not necessarily an answer to say that their political views can be expressed through other members of Parliament of their own political persuasion: there may be some particular local issue that needs to be expressed, but which is unlikely to be expressed – or unlikely to be expressed in the way a large section of that community would like to see it expressed – by the person elected to 'represent' that electorate, and a member for another electorate would fail to create the necessary impact.

There are sections of the community which favour political views that are not represented by any of the major political parties. With the strength of the party machine today, it is unlikely that their views will achieve representation in the House of Commons in the sense of returning a member (and, more significantly, sufficient members) to Parliament. They must necessarily depend, therefore, upon constituting a pressure group to bring pressure upon the party in power. Undoubtedly, pressure groups can and do exert influence far beyond their numbers; but the likelihood of an unsuccessful political party forming a successful pressure group is small. The very fact that that group as a political party has failed to achieve representation would tell strongly against it as a pressure group.

Limitations on the power of private members

In Parliament the government has control of the notice paper or agenda. It is only natural that legislation sponsored by the government should take priority, but this has reached the stage where legislation sponsored by the Opposition or by independent members (or even by back bench members of the governing party) has little chance of being passed into law. Indeed, such proposed legislation has little chance of even being debated. A private member is therefore reduced to working through the party system. The member who rises to ministerial rank has a much better chance of having legislation passed through Parliament; but this, of course, depends on gaining a portfolio the duties of which include being in charge of the relevant department. In order to rise to ministerial rank a back bench member (a backbencher) must be careful not to upset the leaders of the party, and this is likely seriously to restrict activities as a member until ministerial rank is obtained.

There was at one time a system whereby Parliament set aside certain days for private members to bring matters before the House. Even in the 1950s, however, it was noted of Parliament that:

> There are limited opportunities for back bench members to initiate legislation, and some notable social reforms have been brought about by this means; but the days set apart for this are few, there is a ballot at the beginning of each session for priority, and the hazards on the long road to the statute book are many.[1]

Today, the pressure of government business means that even the government's own measures do not get proper debate and the days formerly allotted to private members are usually occupied by the overflow of government business.

A member of Parliament in good standing with the party leaders and the party members in that member's electorate is likely to have no trouble in being put forward as the party candidate at the next election. A member may well represent the same seat for many years. However, if a member offends the party leadership or influential members of the local party branch, party endorsement is likely to be lost and with it the best chance of securing re-election. Most politicians are eager to secure further terms in office. It is strongly in their interests to keep in the favour of their party, even if this means allowing troublesome matters to pass unquestioned. This does not mean that a cynical view should be taken of the role of members of Parliament, but it does mean that there are practical difficulties to a backbencher taking an innovatory role.

---

1   *Everyman's Encyclopaedia*, 5th edn, Bazman EF, 1968, Readers Union and JM Dent & Sons Ltd, London, Vol 9 at 486, under the side heading Parliamentary Bills.

Members of Parliament do play an important role in helping residents of their electorate. A voter who gets into difficulties with a government authority may approach the local member of Parliament with a request for help. A member of Parliament has a better chance of gaining the co-operation of a government department than a private individual would; but even in this regard a member of the ruling party will have a better chance than an independent member or a member of a small party.

There is a conflict between the need of a member of Parliament to spend time in Parliament itself and the need to perform electorate duties. Particularly when the government lacks a substantial majority, members of the major parties are required to be within call when legislation is being considered. The call is made by the ringing of bells within the relevant House, within the precincts, and even within members' homes if sufficiently close. A period of eight minutes is allowed from the time the bells commence ringing until the taking of the vote ends.

Limitations on Parliament's responsiveness to changes in the electorates

Elections are necessarily held infrequently. During the period between elections the opinion of the majority of voters may change. It may therefore be that towards the end of a government's term the majority of the people is opposed to that government's policies. Parliament represents the views of the majority of the electors as at the time at which the members of Parliament were elected (or, more precisely, the views of those electors who made up the majority in the majority of electorates – the disparity in the number of voters in the various electorates can result in a government having a working majority in Parliament although representing less than half the total number of voters in the United Kingdom as a whole. This can happen if one party gains a large majority in a limited number of seats whilst another party gains a small majority in many seats).

In point of fact, no party puts all its intended legislation before the people. It puts forward by way of its election platform those aspects of its policy that it believes will appeal to the voters. Legislation is brought forward from time to time, much of it as a result of departmental proposals. The voters, therefore, have little effective say in legislative policy. Quite apart from this aspect, however, issues arise which were not foreseen by any party at the time of the election. The government may feel that it has to make a decision between which of two sides to a dispute it will support in some other country. The sending of troops to Bosnia is a well-known example. This, of course, had never been an election issue, and the public had no opportunity of expressing an effective view through the electoral system. Whether what was published through the media represented the majority view in the United Kingdom, and whether that view was what was best for the United Kingdom, were questions the government had to determine for itself without the benefit of an answer through the ballot box.

There are those who advocate what is called a right of recall to give the electorate a more effective control. Under this system a specified percentage of voters could require the member for their electorate to stand for re-election notwithstanding that the term of Parliament had not expired. This system has a certain attractiveness, particularly if the member has defected to another party; but in practice it may prove dangerous under United Kingdom conditions. It could lead to great instability. In order to govern effectively a party coming to power has to have several years in which to become experienced in running the machinery of government and in which to pass its legislative programme into law. A member of Parliament has many duties to perform, and should not be constantly under electorate threat. In those electorates which are not safe seats a large number of the voters will normally have voted against the sitting member in any event. Unless a very large majority of the electorate is required to sign a petition for a new election in that electorate, the very people who have failed to unseat the member at the previous election could call an unlimited number of new elections by sending round fresh petitions each time. It is well known how easy it is to obtain signatures to a petition, so that the sitting member, although re-elected each time, would have time for nothing else but defending the local position. This could be particularly disruptive if a minister were the one to be attacked. However, this damage could be minimised by providing that no petition could be lodged until nine months after an election and that no more than one petition could be lodged in each year.

The overwhelming pressure of business which the members of Parliament nowadays have to face makes it very difficult for them to discover what views the community really holds, even in their own electorate. To discover community views, particularly in an electorate in which the population is large, is not a simple or speedy task, and the average member of Parliament is very short of time in which to carry out this duty. This makes the members of Parliament vulnerable to pressure groups which put their own case very strongly and may appear to the member to represent the view of the community. In fact, they may be a very small group who make up for lack of numbers by loudness of noise. A member of Parliament who really wishes to carry out the voters' views may easily be misled by such a group into supporting a policy which is not in accordance with the majority view at all.

Limitations on Parliament as a law-making body

Since the Second World War, Parliament has attempted to regulate many areas of life by legislation. Many of the topics with which it deals are extremely complex, and only a very small minority of the members of Parliament can be expert in any one of these fields. Indeed, Parliament may pass legislation in a field in which none of its members has any expertise. This problem has left Parliament increasingly in the hands of its professional advisers, in this case members of the bureaucracy. The bureaucracy has grown enormously since the Second World War and has itself become a very powerful pressure group. Many Acts of Parliament are directly inspired by government departments. Also, the practice has grown up of dealing with the general subject matter in an

Act of Parliament and leaving the details to be covered by subordinate legislation produced by the bureaucracy or by statutory authorities.

The individual member of Parliament may find great difficulty in even understanding a Bill covering some complex and technical field; and, even if foreseeing problems likely to arise as a result of the Bill being passed into law as an Act, it is unlikely that there would be time in a parliamentary debate to raise the matter and obtain a detailed discussion. If an amendment is produced to meet the problem it may have to be drafted in haste; and, despite the best efforts of the drafter, it may prove to be inconsistent with some other section of the Act, or it may prove not to meet the particular complexities that have given rise to it.

Parliament's sources of information

Parliaments do not rely merely on the general knowledge of their members and on the expert advice coming from the bureaucracy. There are methods which Parliaments can use to obtain information in great detail on specific subjects. Of course, information may be fed to the government from various pressure groups, and from various sections of the community likely to be affected by the legislation. Information may also be fed to the government from other governments.

There are certain established procedures by which Parliament seeks to inform itself on specific matters of concern to it. The most favoured method is that of the parliamentary committee to carry out specific functions. An enquiry conducted by such a committee differs in important respects from an enquiry conducted by a court of law or by a royal commission. The members of the committee are free to come and go as they please. A member may hear little or much of the evidence that is given. Members may decide, not on the evidence placed before them, but on popular reaction or on representations from within their own electorates. They may decide on political principles. They are not bound by the rules of practice, procedure or evidence that bind the courts; and their decisions are open neither to challenge nor to appeal. Unless the particular matter has become the subject of public outcry, a government department or statutory authority is likely to be at a substantial advantage as against members of the public at such an enquiry.

Another alternative adopted by Parliament is that of a royal commission. Sometimes the person appointed to conduct such an enquiry is appointed as a board of enquiry instead of a royal commission, but there is no material difference so far as informing Parliament is concerned. The person conducting the enquiry (whatever its technical title) is given terms of reference setting out the scope of the enquiry to be conducted. Those terms of reference limit the extent of the enquiry.

CHAPTER 20

LIMITATIONS ON THE EFFECTIVENESS OF SUBORDINATE LAW-MAKING BODIES

The nature of subordinate law-making bodies

Subordinate law-making bodies vary widely in nature and in composition. Local government bodies are composed of elected representatives assisted by professional officers. They have limited powers to make subordinate legislation.

Government departments, most of which have the right to produce subordinate legislation, are composed of professional civil servants and, whilst they may receive representations from the community, will make their own decision about what subordinate legislation is necessary without requiring the approval of any local community. Of course, the subordinate legislation may be produced as a result of knowledge gained by inspectors on the departmental staff who in the course of their duties inspect premises of the nature of those to which the subordinate legislation is to apply. Another means by which the department may gain information of a practical nature is by constituting a committee with members drawn not only from the departmental staff but from members of the community actually engaged in the activity which is to be controlled by the subordinate legislation.

Statutory authorities are bodies of a semi-governmental nature constituted by Acts of Parliament. Most of these bodies have no local representation upon them.

Difficulties in producing effective subordinate legislation

Subject to the controls and requirements of the European Community an Act of Parliament may deal with any topic Parliament pleases. It has been said that it can do everything except make a man into a woman or a woman into a man – it has to leave that to medical practitioners! The powers of subordinate law-making bodies are more limited. In the case of a statutory authority it is normally given power only over a particular field with which that authority is constituted to deal. Similarly, a government department has no right to make subordinate legislation on any topic that it pleases, but only on such topics as have been entrusted to it by Parliament.

It is not sufficient for a subordinate law-making body to choose a topic and regulate it for the public good. The body must choose a topic which is within its powers; and, in dealing with that topic, it must not go beyond the limits of the power given to it by Parliament. If it does go beyond those limits, no matter how wise or beneficial its scheme may be, that scheme is invalid (sometimes to the extent of the excess beyond its powers, but sometimes altogether). A subordinate law-making body is often required by Parliament to follow a specific procedure in making its subordinate legislation. If it fails to follow the relevant procedure then, even though it had power to deal with the topic, the subordinate legislation it has made may well be held to be invalid.

A subordinate law-making body, in making laws for the fields entrusted to its care by Parliament, not only has to be careful that it stays within its powers and follows the correct procedure – it must also consider very carefully the practical effects of the legislation it wishes to produce. It is very easy for a mistake in drafting, or a failure to foresee all the practical problems involved, to create difficulties which the authority had never intended.

One other difficulty in subordinate legislation is worthy of comment. It can, perhaps, readily be seen that the same topic may be dealt with by different local government councils in different ways. This may produce problems for a company whose activities extend through several local government areas.

CHAPTER 21

LIMITATIONS ON THE EFFECTIVENESS OF COURTS

Lack of knowledge of legal rights

Most members of the community have never made a study of their legal rights, or of the legal system. They may know, in general terms, some of the major provisions of the criminal law, and they may know of the negligence action as used to gain damages, but they are most unlikely to have any detailed knowledge of our legal system and of their rights within it. They are even more unlikely to know of the present state of those parts of our law which are developing and expanding.

What does such a person know of the rights conferred by the doctrine of legitimate expectations or of the rights available if there is an abuse of public office? The time limits prescribed by Parliament for instituting legal proceedings vary according to the nature of the proceedings being instituted, and that is hardly likely to be a topic of conversation across the breakfast table. There are few, if any, such persons who would make a habit of reading the weekly outpouring of superior court decisions to be found in the various series of law reports. Then, too, there are rights conferred by statute: the lay person may have heard of the name of the statute, but what of all the amendments, many of which are to be found tucked away in sections part way through a statute of another name[1] or in a schedule to such a statute?[2] It is not enough for a litigant in person to come before the court with a lengthy statement of facts and say 'I want damages': those whom that litigant has sued have rights, too, including the right to know what legal remedy is being relied upon. Rights may indeed exist, but the court can only enforce rights if the matter is brought to the court's attention in properly constituted proceedings.

If a statutory authority gives notice that it is going to exercise statutory powers to the detriment of a landowner, how is the landowner to know that that notice is invalid (whether as being beyond the powers of the authority or as failing to comply with the statutory procedure)? The litigant who seeks to enforce legal rights (whether conferred by statute, or created by contract, or developed by common law) without the aid of a lawyer is likely to be at a serious disadvantage. Unfortunately, not only is there the impossibility of persons untrained in law knowing the law, but there is also the problem that legal proceedings must be started, if at all, within the periods prescribed by Parliament (or, in some cases, within an extended period when Parliament has conferred power upon a court to extend the period – a power that is not conferred generally by Parliament).

---

1   The person whose land has been the subject of compulsory purchase (that is, expropriation) may find the Acquisition of Land Act 1981, but would such a person know to refer to s 579(1) Housing Act 1985 which in relevant circumstances renders the Acquisition of Land Act 1981 inapplicable?

2   Section 4(4)(e) Local Government, Planning and Land Act 1980 was amended by Schedule 8 Transport Act.

Lack of preparedness to use the court system

Most people become personally involved with our court system only very rarely throughout their entire lives. Many people never become involved with it at all, or only a very few times for motoring offences or when they are called up for jury service. Litigation is often a lengthy and expensive process which most people would avoid if at all possible. The unfamiliar courtroom scene may create a mystique which is likely to increase people's nervousness of going before the courts at all. Most people have a natural preference for settling their disputes privately rather than facing the uncertainty, delay and expense of a court action. Indeed, it is very much to the advantage of the community if disputes can be settled privately, but sensibly. The court system is used to settle those disputes which cannot be settled sensibly in any other way, and to lay down principles on which people can base their future conduct. However, there are many cases in which people who have an undoubted right to go to court and claim damages from someone else prefer not to do so, even at the expense of their legal rights. Whatever the system of law adopted, it is likely that that would continue to be a fact of life. Perhaps it can not unfairly be said that for the average member of the community, going to court is not unlike going to the headmaster's study.

Limitations arising from the cost of litigation

One of the problems of the modern age is the cost of services. Anyone who owns a washing machine is well aware of the cost of a service call even for the most trivial work. The washing machine technician has undergone a comparatively short period of training. The lawyer, on the other hand, has undergone a lengthy period of training and is likely to have spent a minimum of eight years longer in training than the washing machine technician. Not only has the lawyer lost the whole of those years from his or her earning life and had to bear (or the parents have had to bear) the cost of maintaining the student during that period, but the rate of pay during the early years in the legal profession will be less than that of a secretary in the same office. The lawyer's earning life, therefore, is comparatively short. Moreover, the responsibilities carried by the lawyer are heavy. The ethical standards of the legal profession expect its members not only to remember the law that they learned in the course of professional training, but to keep themselves abreast of the mass of new law that is constantly appearing. Every person rendering a service must of course keep abreast of new developments, but the lawyer is faced with a greater volume of new material than most other callings. In addition, the library that the lawyer needs to develop both in the office and at home is expensive to buy and to maintain. The combination of all these factors makes the provision of legal services expensive for the client who has to pay for them.

The person whose assets or earnings are enough to preclude legal aid but whose assets are not such as to come within the concept of 'wealthy' can undoubtedly find litigation, and particularly litigation in the superior courts, an expensive experience. The cost of litigation does deter many people in this major group of the community from enforcing their legal rights.

Limitations caused by delay

A particularly unfortunate feature of our legal system is the delays that plague it. It is natural that, except in the most urgent cases, a person seeking to come before the court should take a place in the queue. Also, there are preliminary matters to be attended to before the case can be brought on before a judge, or before a judge and jury. It is necessary to file a statement of claim (and, in the superior courts, further documents known as 'pleadings') to define the kind of claim which is being made and opposed. However, there are many opportunities for excessive delay by one or both of the parties to litigation.

There are undoubtedly means by which the present procedures could be speeded up. The courts have introduced new measures to speed up the processes. However, it is a matter of concern that many of the delays are due not to the processes and procedures of the legal system but to lack of sufficient courts and judges. If a person subjected to litigation is told that it will take 18 months or two years for the case to be heard, it is no consolation for that person to be told that others are suffering the same delays.

The most worrying delays are those occurring in the enforcement of the criminal law. If an accused person is refused bail, or if the accused person is unable to provide the security required as a condition of the granting of bail, the only answer provided by the community is to place that person in gaol until the time of trial. At trial it may happen that the accused is acquitted or is granted a bond, yet that accused may have served months of imprisonment on remand whilst awaiting trial. This situation is all the worse when regard is had to the fact that in legal theory under our system of justice (as distinct from the continental system of justice) every person accused of a crime is deemed to be innocent until such time as found guilty by a court of law (save in respect of certain exceptional offences created by statute).

In civil cases a further problem of delay occurs at the end of the case. Of course, in many cases the judge is able to give a decision immediately; but there is a significant percentage of cases in which the judge has to withhold the decision (or, as it is called in law, 'reserve' the decision). The judge reserves a decision so as to research and review the law. There is much to be said for the view that there should be spare judges available so that, the moment a judge has heard a case, that judge can start on researching and writing the judgment in that case instead of having to start on hearing the next case.

Delays in the courts also affect the parties and their witnesses in another way. If a person makes an appointment to see an accountant, there is rightly an expectation to see that accountant on the day and at, or at least close to, the time nominated. An appointment with a court, however, may result in a hearing commencing days or even weeks after the appointed day. The cause of the delay is to be found in the impossibility of telling just how long any particular case will take. The case or cases preceding that particular case may take considerably longer than has been allowed for them. Again, it would be to the advantage of the community if there were spare judges who could take up the hearing of any case that was delayed in such a way. Parties and their witnesses need to know when a case will be heard rather than have to suffer periods, often lengthy periods, of uncertainty.

It is well known that even immediately after a motor accident the various witnesses to that accident are likely to tell different stories. This is not because some of the witnesses are lying, but because they saw the accident from different positions and in some cases heard, rather than saw, the accident. In one case in which there were six witnesses, three gave sworn evidence that one car was proceeding forward at a fast rate of speed, one gave sworn evidence that it was proceeding forward in first gear, a fifth gave sworn evidence that it was stationary, and a sixth gave sworn evidence that it was going in reverse: the probability is that none of those witnesses was lying, but that each, or most, had merely heard the sound of the collision, looked quickly around and seen the position the cars were then in, and had automatically reconstructed in their minds what they thought must have occurred. Within a very short space of time it would be difficult to separate out in their minds what they had actually seen and what they had automatically reconstructed. The longer the delay in getting a case before the court, the worse this problem is likely to become. Cross-examination provides a useful method of testing a witness's evidence; but, the longer the lapse of time between the accident and the court trial, the less accurate and the less detailed the witness's memory is likely to become: those things merely thought to have been seen may well come to take priority in the witness's mind, without any evil intention, over what was actually seen, and it may be almost impossible to separate one from the other.

When a case is taken on appeal to a higher court, it is necessary once again for the litigant to place the case in the queue – in this case, not the queue for the original court hearing, but the queue for a hearing on appeal. Also, there is the documentation that has to be prepared for the court hearing the appeal. If the hearing of the case before the original court involved the taking of evidence, that evidence will have to be typed out so that the judges composing the appellate court can study whatever aspects of that evidence are involved in the appeal. All the documents placed before the original court also have to be copied for the judges composing the appellate court.

An example of delay is afforded by a case in which the writ was issued on 26 October 1976. On 13 April 1981 the writ was ordered by a master of the court to be amended. The case was heard and decided in May 1983, and an appeal was heard and decided in February 1984 – a period of seven years and four months after the issue of the writ.[3]

Delays do not necessarily cease even after a court has handed down its judgment. If damages have been awarded, it is unlikely that the party who has to pay will have the cash available in court, and it is quite likely that the unsuccessful party will not have enough money in the bank to be able to write out a cheque. In such a case, steps have to be taken to collect the money and, if necessary, to sell up the assets of the defendant in order to obtain the money owing. This process may in itself take a long time, and it is of course not in the interests of the party who has to pay to speed matters along.

---

3   *Thames Guaranty Ltd v Campbell* [1985] QB 210.

Speedy hearings in urgent cases

The consideration of delays to this point can give a misleading picture. What has been examined is the ordinary case. When a case is urgent and the parties to the action are prepared to treat it urgently, the courts can certainly provide a speedy service. How speedily a really urgent case may be heard and decided in the English courts is exemplified by a matter in which a case was heard, an appeal from the decision in the case was heard by the Court of Appeal on a Saturday, and a further appeal from the decision on that first appeal was heard and decided all within a week.

Unavailability of the court system

Our legal system places strict limits on who may become a plaintiff or a defendant, a prosecutor or an accused. Only 'legal persons' are allowed to be parties to an action before a court. A man or a company can sue; a tree, a dog, or a social group or unincorporated society cannot. An unincorporated group may be vitally affected as a group by the results of a court action; but as the group is not a legal person, it cannot appear either by one of its members or by counsel to advance or to defend those interests. Such a group can, of course, incorporate (that is, become a company) provided that it has the money and the desire to do so; but, although incorporation can be achieved very quickly, it may be too late for the benefit of the group in the particular circumstances, for the need to commence the litigation may have arisen before incorporation can be achieved.

Even when the would-be litigant is a legal person, this does not automatically entitle that person to bring a case before the court. To be allowed to be a litigant that person must have an interest in the action which our legal system is willing to recognise as one giving 'legal standing'. For example, in a case involving a 'public nuisance' it is not enough that a person has suffered damage because of this public nuisance: the would-be plaintiff must have suffered more damage than that suffered by the members of the general public. If a highway authority closes a road unlawfully, that is a public nuisance. A householder may suffer inconvenience (and, in that sense, damage) by having to divert to reach home instead of going directly as would have been the case if the road had not been closed, but the damage suffered in that way is a damage shared by the members of the public generally and is not enough to give legal standing to challenge the road closure.

A further problem arises because of the technicality of certain remedies. Parliament has intervened to attempt to reduce legal technicalities, but the problem still remains. Particularly in the case of the older remedies it is necessary, not merely to have a good legal case, but to choose the correct remedy and to make sure that all the technicalities have been complied with. If this is not done, the litigant may well find that the remedy sought is not available in the case. The most notorious for their technicalities are what are known as the prerogative writs – the writs of *mandamus* (to compel a person or statutory authority to perform a legal duty), the writ of *prohibition* (to prohibit a statutory authority or a judicial body of lower status than the court issuing the writ from doing something it is prohibited in law from doing), the writ of *certiorari* (to challenge the correctness of proceedings in a lower court or other body), the writ of *quo warranto* (to challenge the validity of the holding of public office by the defendant), and the writ of *habeas corpus* (to challenge the validity of the imprisonment, or the validity of imprisonment in a particular place, of the person bringing the proceedings). To meet the problems caused by the technicalities of the prerogative writs the remedy by way of judicial review has been developed. This remedy, too, has its limitations. Thus, it is only in 'exceptional circumstances' that a court will grant judicial review if the applicant 'has not exhausted established appeal procedures'.[4]

---

4   *R v Deputy Governor of Parkhurst Prison ex p Hague* [1990] 3 WLR 1210, Taylor LJ (later Lord Taylor of Gosforth CJ) at 1259; affirmed without considering this aspect, [1992] 11 AC 58.

CHAPTER 22

LIMITATIONS ON THE EFFECTIVENESS OF THE COMMON LAW

The courts rely on the litigant

The courts of law are not able to pronounce on any topic which takes their fancy. They are required to consider those cases, and only those cases, which some person brings before them. The courts have consistently refused to give opinions on hypothetical cases – that is, cases which have not yet come up as a dispute between parties.[1] In most cases the concern of the judge is not with elaborating new broad principles or doctrines of the law but in deciding the particular issues which have come before the court. The common law develops gradually from case to case; and, the more frequently cases in a particular field come before the courts, the more opportunity there is for development of the law in that field. The number of cases coming before the courts in a particular field of law depends not on the whim of the judges, or on what they think is important or interesting, but on what is important to the particular litigants involved. This helps to ensure that the courts concentrate on those issues which are most important to that section of the general public which is prepared to engage in litigation.

The fact that the courts are dependent upon litigants bringing matters before them is well illustrated by the development of the doctrine of abuse of public office. This is a doctrine which enables a citizen to recover damages if suffering loss as a result of abuse of powers by a public official. It was a doctrine applied by the courts in 19th-century England, but it lay dormant for almost a century until litigation involving the application of the doctrine arose in 1957.[2] The doctrine was there, and available to any litigant, during the whole of that century that elapsed, but the courts had no means of developing the doctrine during that period because no case was brought before them involving it.

Common law principles affected by statute

Parliament, of course, has the power to override even the most basic of common law principles. For example, Parliament can provide that the right of an accused not to answer questions which might incriminate is taken away in a particular case. Acts of Parliament relating to taxation may compel the individual to answer questions, and may make it a criminal offence to refuse to do so. The courts, however, will protect these fundamental principles of the common law so far as possible by requiring any taking away of those rights to be by plain words.

Parliament may affect the development of common law principles not by encroaching upon them but by fossilising them. For example, the law on sale of goods was developed by the common law and later enshrined in Acts of

---

1   *Sumner v William Henderson & Sons* [1963] 1 WLR 823.

2   *Wood v Blair and Helmsley Rural District Council* (1957) 4 ALR 243.

Parliament. These Acts were not changed substantially for about a century. During that period the form of typical commercial transactions did change, with much greater need for consumer protection. Because the law was codified in Acts of Parliament the courts were unable to change or greatly to improve it. Had the law been set out wholly in the earlier decisions of the courts, they could well have been able to develop the law to meet the changing needs of the community as was done, for example, in the growth of the law of negligence. The law of negligence had always been part of the common law, but in 1932 a decision of the House of Lords[3] gave its applicability a very much widened scope by making the test of liability in negligence the test of 'who is my neighbour?' Similarly, the law relating to the duty owed by the occupier of land to persons (even trespassers) who come onto the occupier's land has expanded to meet changing needs by developing the new test of common humanity. In a decision given in 1972 Lord Morris was able to say that 'it is today basic to our legal thinking that every member of a community must have regard to the effect upon others of his actions or inactions ... Why and for what reasons should the Railways Board owe ... any duty at all ...? I would answer for reasons of common sense and common humanity'.[4] That was not a sudden change on the part of the courts, but a change that had been developing in the decisions. As Lord Reid pointed out in *Herrington's case*,[5] 'a new chapter opened with *Videan v British Transport Commission*'.[6] The House of Lords in *Herrington's case* wrote further in that new chapter.

Conservatism on the Bench

Our legal system provides for the judges to be chosen from among experienced members of the legal profession. They are not normally young, and the legal profession itself has tended to be more conservative than the bulk of the community. There are many judges who, while giving a very sound technical interpretation of the law, do not see it as their business to advance the law or press for reform through their decisions in particular cases.

When an attempt is being made to open up a new field of the law, or to extend an existing field, the conservatism or otherwise of the judges who have first to hear the relevant cases can be vital. In such cases, where the law has not yet crystallised, it is open to the judges to decide either in favour of expanding the law or of restricting it within its present boundaries. It could not be said that a judgment either way would be contrary to the authorities or contrary to law. Because of the doctrine of precedent, the way in which the first few cases are decided is likely to prove decisive of the way in which that aspect of the law will develop, at least for a substantial time to come.

There are judges who have deliberately attempted to expand the law as far as possible in those fields where they feel that this is necessary or desirable. The

---

3   *Donoghue v Stevenson* [1932] AC 562.

4   *British Railways Board v Herrington* [1972] AC 877 at 906.

5   *British Railways Board v Herrington* [1972] AC 877.

6   [1963] 2 QB 650.

most notable of these judges in modern times is undoubtedly Lord Denning MR (the judge who presided over the Court of Appeal). For many years Lord Denning attempted to reform and expand the law through the cases which came before the Court of Appeal to be decided. Unfortunately, on some occasions Lord Denning showed little respect for earlier precedents, even those decided by the House of Lords which are binding on the Court of Appeal, and of course binding on its constituent judges. The result has been, in a number of cases, that instead of the law being expanded it was actually restricted by the reaction of the court (the House of Lords) hearing appeals from Denning judgments. In overturning what they regarded as too radical departures from established law, they have in some instances at least swung the pendulum unnecessarily far in the opposite direction. This period of conflict between Lord Denning and the judges of the House of Lords illustrates how essential it is that the law be developed by evolution and not by revolution: what develops gradually and progressively is accepted, but a sudden break with previous legal principles, doctrines and precedents, though sometimes successful, is more likely to prove unacceptable.

The very fact that Parliament has intervened on a large scale to reform the law has been used by some of the more conservative judges as a reason not to perform the same function themselves. On many occasions judges have said that, if major changes are needed, it should be left to Parliament to carry out those changes. This is unfortunate because it is the judges who have the greatest knowledge of the existing state of the law and of its defects and who have the opportunity, when developing a new line of authority, to view a suggested new principle of law as it relates to various fact situations before a final decision is made to adopt it as part of our law.

CHAPTER 23

LIMITATIONS ON THE ENFORCEMENT OF LAW

Lack of community knowledge of the law

Even experienced professional lawyers find it very difficult to keep up with the rapid development of the law, and in particular with the flood of statutes and subordinate legislation. It cannot be expected of ordinary citizens that they would become familiar with the details of the multitudinous statutes and statutory instruments which have been laid down to govern life today. Even in regard to the road rules, which are probably among the best known of subordinate legislation, there are very few people who could fairly claim familiarity with them in their current form and detail. Even those who have recently obtained a driving licence have no real means of knowing which of the subordinate legislation provisions have been altered since. Despite this, ignorance of the law is no excuse; and a person who fails to obey the law because of a lack of knowledge of what it requires is nevertheless guilty.

Lack of community acceptance of particular laws

There have been laws which are generally ignored by the public. The most notorious example is the law banning sale of alcoholic liquor in the United States of America. During the period in which prohibition was in force, law-breaking by members of the public was open and flagrant; and such was the demand for illegal liquor that organised crime was able to expand greatly. It is inevitable that as conditions and the attitudes of society change, some laws which have long been on the statute book become outmoded, but there may at first be no great demand for change. Such laws may merely not be enforced. If the attempt is made to enforce them, those officers of the law who are attempting to do so will find that they meet with passive resistance: people will not report breaches, and juries will refuse to convict.

Any motorist must be well aware of the fact that by far the majority of drivers using the motorways exceed the speed limit. In a check made over several weeks in 1995 the number ignoring the speed limit on the M40 was over 90% of all drivers, a percentage that has been rising since at least 1985.

It has been said that the average person will in any event accord with what the law requires except when behind the wheel of a motor car. There is, however, a dangerous aspect to lack of enforcement of the law that is not widely recognised in the community. Once it becomes generally accepted in the community that a particular law can be broken with impunity, the effects of that law-breaking do not stop there. It is a simple step from the breaking of one law to the breaking of others. Without realising it many individuals within the community become judges in their own cause, determining which laws are there to be broken. Such a course can rapidly bring the law into disrepute, and that can only be to the disadvantage of the community. Respect for the law is essential to the stability of the community the law serves.

Limited detection of offences and offenders

Not every offence that is committed is reported to the police. How often has a motorist, condemning the offences being committed by a driver ahead, wished to have a police cap and police powers? How seldom has that motorist reported those offences to the police? The factors that lead to failure to report offenders are many. Some of those factors are a feeling that there is little chance of the offender being caught (the police can trace the car, but who was driving?), resistance to the time – perhaps days – that would be taken in court proceedings, and a wish not to be 'involved'. The police keep statistics of the offences which have been reported to them, and of the proportion of those offences in which a conviction has been obtained, but no statistics can be provided for the proportion of offences which have never been reported to the police.

Not every offence which is reported to the police ends in a conviction. There are naturally occasions on which there is insufficient evidence to convict anybody, or when the jury feels that the case has not been proved beyond reasonable doubt. There are also cases in which the police are unable to obtain enough evidence even to launch a prosecution. The resources available to the police are limited, and our community would not have it otherwise: the thought of a policeman standing behind every person's back is one which our community would find intolerable. Yet it is only by that means that every person who committed an offence could be brought to trial and convicted.

Government as protecting itself from the law

It has always been the case that government has had special privileges. In medieval times the courts were in reality the King's courts and he not only could not be prosecuted in them, he could not even be sued in a civil case. The legal doctrine was that 'The King can do no wrong'. Even today there is a presumption in interpreting a statute that the Crown is not bound by the provisions of that statute unless by express words or by necessary implication.

The Crown has long had a privilege, taken advantage of by the government and by government departments, of withholding certain documents which it claims it is not in the public interest to reveal. There was a time when the courts would accept the certificate of a minister to that effect as final and conclusive, but nowadays the courts are prepared to balance the conflicting interests of litigant and public. Even that balancing of interests, however, can well result in the litigant who is suing the government or a government instrumentality being placed at a disadvantage by comparison with a litigant suing an ordinary member of the community. When suing an individual, or a company, or even a statutory body that is not protected by the Crown privilege, the litigant is entitled to inspect, copy and tender as evidence all relevant documents over which the person, company or body being sued has control unless those documents are protected by, for example, professional privilege (such as documents containing legal advice given to that party by that party's own lawyers for the purpose of preparing a defence). The government, however, can rely upon Crown privilege to exclude documents from those it has to produce even though by doing so it deprives the litigant of documents necessary to prove the case against the government.

Government, semi-government and statutory authorities are much larger and more powerful than private individuals or small groups. They have the resources to fight a case through a series of appeals. Also, they have the prestige given them by their position of authority, and they are likely to be able to obtain the ear of the government of the day. These factors make it more difficult to enforce the law against a government, semi-government or statutory authority than it is to enforce that same law against private individuals and companies. It can be noted, for example, that many of the most flagrant breaches of the environment protection laws are committed not by individuals or companies but by statutory bodies which are themselves given statutory powers to enforce the law as against other people. The bad example that this sets is likely to have a serious effect on respect for the law amongst ordinary people.

CHAPTER 24

THE CHANGING ROLE OF THE LEGAL PROFESSION

Attempts to exclude lawyers

There are those in the community who are suspicious of lawyers and what they regard as legalism. They believe that justice without lawyers would be speedier and cheaper. In certain specialised fields they have managed to achieve the establishment of tribunals before which lawyers do not have a monopoly of practice or in which lawyers are prohibited from appearing at all. One hopes that these same people, if suffering from appendicitis, would not propose that their operation should be carried out by people not qualified as doctors, but they have managed to deprive people not used to presenting their own cases of the benefit of the assistance of those trained specifically for the role.

In practice, where lawyers and non-lawyers are allowed to appear before a person conducting a hearing,[1] the lawyer has a tremendous advantage as does the client. Even where the opponent is a professional, trained perhaps as an engineer or as a town planner, that opponent's training does not include training in how to present a case before a court, or in the legal points which inevitably occur. Such hearings are bound to apply the laws of the land, and the courts can quash their decisions if they fail to conform to those laws.

Attempts to exclude the courts

Attempts to exclude the courts have been more widespread than attempts to exclude lawyers. Lawyers are able to appear before many hearings which are not within the ordinary court system. Such specialised hearings may well have lawyers occupying the position normally occupied by a judge, and Parliament may require those lawyers to have all the qualifications that it prescribes for a judge. Many of the hearings are in cases involving amounts of money which are larger than those normally dealt with even in the superior courts.

In the field of commercial disputes, business executives often specify in their contracts for arbitration before, or instead of, a court hearing. Lawyers appear on both sides before the arbitrator, and many of the arbitrators are themselves lawyers. Such hearings tend to be lengthy and expensive, and may well result in an attempt to have the arbitrator's decision overturned by the superior courts. The real problem is that many commercial matters are complex and the issues cannot be decided without a lengthy hearing: at the same time, delay can be enormously expensive for business executives who are subject to interest charges and who have money tied up awaiting the outcome.

---

1   See, for example, the system of hearings by departmental inspectors, and occasionally others outside the public service, provided for in s 114 and Schedule 20 Environment Act 1995. The same applies to town planning appeals. Such hearings under the Town and Country Planning Act 1971 are in the region of 20,000 a year. In most cases the decision is made by the inspector, but in some cases the Secretary of State makes the decision and even overrules the inspector's recommendation.

The fact that these specialised hearings, and the resort to arbitration, exist, points to a failing on the part of our legal system. In particular, it points to the need for speedier justice. It does not, however, point to a successful replacement for our legal system.

In point of fact, the systems of hearings and of arbitration create traps of their own. There are specialised rules governing the manner in which and the extent to which the decision of an arbitrator or a person conducting a hearing can be challenged. The litigant who finds it necessary to challenge the decision of a person who has conducted a hearing (or the Secretary of State) may be more restricted in the points that could be put to the appellate court than would be the case if the appeal were from a court. The procedure that the litigant is forced into by way of appeal is often a more expensive and lengthier procedure than the procedure applying in an appeal from a court.

The extension of the legal profession into new fields

As Parliament opens up new fields of law, so the legal profession has expanded its activities to cover them. Quite a number of important new fields of law have been opened up by Parliament since the Second World War, environment law being a striking example. Each of these fields now provides not merely occasional work for members of the legal profession but specialised fields in which certain members of the legal profession generally spend a great deal of their time.

There are fields of law which require the lawyers advising clients in them to obtain a specialised knowledge outside their knowledge of the law itself. For example, advice involving international loan transactions requires a practical knowledge of the international money market as well as a knowledge of the applicable law: the lawyer who does not possess such knowledge may give advice which would be perfectly sound legally but would lead to unfortunate results. Similarly, the lawyer practising in the field of town planning law must build a sufficient knowledge of the practical workings out of the client's business or other activities: having adequate practical knowledge is essential, for a lack of it may result in the lawyer not appreciating that gaining a grant of planning permission can be rendered worthless by the conditions imposed on the grant. These two examples are from recent developments of the law, but the development of specialised practical knowledge is something that has been required of lawyers for a long time. The lawyer practising in the field of motor accident law must necessarily be aware of the practical situation that an injury to a human joint can lead to osteoarthritis.

The examples we have cited are not intended to suggest that the lawyer must achieve the knowledge of an expert in fields other than the law, but they do point to and illustrate the need for the lawyer to develop a practical expertise outside the field of law. Because lawyers are trained to select rapidly and clearly the essential points of a large mass of material, and to retain those points in mind for as long as they are needed, they are well equipped to develop the necessary expertise and knowledge.

The great increase in government regulation of industry and commerce has led to an expansion in the number of lawyers directly involved with business. Many of the larger companies now have lawyers permanently employed as members of their staff. These lawyers are known as corporate or 'in-house' lawyers. They are people who have practised as barristers or solicitors, and the experience they have gained on the way is of importance to the company whose staff they join. Some of them then spend their lifetime on the staff of a company; others leave the company after a period of years and return to practising as a barrister or in a firm of solicitors.

CHAPTER 25

CHANGE AND THE LAW

The law has always been changing

There has been no period in our legal history when the law has remained completely static. The pace of change has varied over the centuries, but society itself has changed and the legal needs of society have changed with it. The law, while it has seldom found itself in advance of this type of change, has been able to a large degree to develop new doctrines and to expand old ones to meet society's needs.

The method which the common law has used is that of evolution. The judges, in the main, have not attempted to make any radical break with the past, but rather to develop general principles out of isolated cases or lines of authority already in existence. In this way the judges have been able to advance gradually, testing the new doctrine or principle at each point against a variety of fact situations. Our legal system has been relatively free from great swings of doctrine in response to the pendulum of social mores. In each period of our history there have been basic social beliefs, and the law has gone some way towards incorporating these within its structure. However, social mores change, and the law, not having gone the full way towards satisfying temporary demands, will find it easier to change in response to changes in society and its needs.

Our law has always been responsive to some degree to outside influence. It has, in fact, absorbed many streams which originally had different approaches to social problems and a separate court structure: for example, mercantile law, ecclesiastical law, and equity. Today the law is having to adapt to the new demands of the European Community and the provisions of the treaty by which the Member States of that community are bound.

The general acceptability of our legal system

Every legal system has faced the problem of criminals. Ours is no exception in this respect and indeed is troubled by organised crime on a larger scale and a more highly organised basis than was the case earlier in this century. The fact that criminals exist is not in itself a criticism of any particular legal system, because criminals have existed under every legal system which has been tried. A murder is mentioned even in the Book of Genesis.[1] The fact remains that while criminals are a nuisance, and at times a serious nuisance, the existence of crime and criminals does not prevent the continued and satisfactory operation of the legal system.

Whilst individuals may complain of a decision they have lost or of the delays of the law they have experienced, the majority of the community obviously regards the legal system as an adequate and satisfactory safeguard

---

1   *The Bible*, Genesis 4: 8.

for it. The very fact that criticisms are made in particular cases in which an unsuccessful litigant believes that the court has gone wrong is an indication of the general belief that impartial justice is a right to which all members of our society are entitled. There are many societies in the world today of which this could not truthfully be said. Our legal system has for centuries attempted to protect the rights of the citizens even as against the government – a situation which would be unthinkable under many of the tyrannical regimes existing in other parts of the world today. Many of the fundamental principles of our law have been developed specifically to protect the rights of the citizen – for example, the right not to incriminate oneself, the right to trial by jury in most serious cases, the right to freedom from arrest or search of person or property without a lawful warrant, and the right not to have one's property taken without due process of law. There is just cause for public dissatisfaction with the delays, and to a lesser extent with the expense, of the legal process; but most of the doctrines and principles applied by the courts are suited to conditions in modern society. Whilst plenty of room for criticism remains, our legal system is sufficiently adapted to our needs that any radical change proposed should be examined very carefully, to ensure that in reforming a particular abuse some important safeguard is not inadvertently destroyed.

The comparative effectiveness of various methods of changing the law

In any society there are some changes in the law which in practice could not be achieved no matter what means were used. The effectiveness of the various methods of changing the law depends in large part on the kind of society in which change is sought. Under a dictatorship, peaceful means and rational argument are likely to be useless. In order to make an impression on a government which refuses to listen to reason, the adoption of passive resistance or even of violence may be the only ways by which a majority may be able to ensure that its views are heard. Any such attempt, under a dictatorship, is likely to be met by the most stringent and repressive measures.

In a democratic society, where free speech is regarded as a fundamental right, it is much easier for those who wish to change the law to convince the public and the government by reasoned argument. It is also much easier to attempt to achieve change by means of demonstrations or other forms of protest. Pressure groups with media publicity have been able to exercise considerable influence over politicians – often out of all proportion to the actual numbers of their members.

The individual who seeks to obtain a change in the law can do so by making representations to a Secretary of State, a minister, a member of Parliament, a government department, a statutory authority or the members or officers of a council. How effective those representations will be will depend in large part on whether approaches are made to the right person, and on whether there is any government policy opposed to the change which is sought in the law. It will also depend upon whether the proposed change is attractive to the political convictions of the party in power and attractive to the philosophy of the department or other authority that would be affected by the change. An important factor, of course, would be the standing in the community of the person seeking the change. A newspaper editor, for instance, would have a much greater chance of achieving a particular change than would an employee on the factory floor.

Representations by an individual to a council need not be confined to changes in the subordinate legislation made by that council. Such an individual may very well seek to obtain the support of a council for changes in the law made by Parliament or changes in the law made by way of subordinate legislation at departmental level. If the council is convinced of the correctness of the proposal, it can add its weight by way of representations to the local members of Parliament. Representations may be made to a Secretary of State, a minister, a shadow minister or a member of Parliament by speaking to him or her personally at Westminster in the large circular area known as the lobby. It is from that term that the word lobbying is derived.

If a number of individuals agree in seeking a particular change in the law, they are able to form themselves into a pressure group. Such a group, instead of acting as individuals, works together to achieve the change which its members desire. It can make representations in exactly the same way as the private individual, but can do so by means of a deputation or by means of media publicity. The result is that the leaders of the group can state quite correctly that they are speaking for a larger number of committed supporters and their utterances may be taken at political level as utterances on behalf of a much greater segment of the community than is in fact the case. If six people approach a minister as a deputation, how is the minister to know whether they represent a group of 12 people or a group of 1,200? If they appear to be convinced and confident, and if that group has achieved publicity through the media, the minister may well be led into a belief that the group has an influence well beyond its actual influence in the community. Even when the majority of the community is opposed to the change which the pressure group wants, the pressure group is dedicated to achieving that change and is vocal in its support of that change; the majority of the community, whilst not liking the change, has many more important things to do than speaking up on every issue which is raised, and in fact has far less opportunity of making its voice heard than has the much smaller but highly organised and vocal pressure group.

When a pressure group has the support of considerable numbers, or has a small group of supporters who dominate a small area and are concerned with a local issue (such as the closing of a street to through traffic), it is possible for that group to organise a demonstration. A large crowd may march, or a small group including most of the local residents may attempt to block their street or to keep it open. Such demonstrations attract much greater media publicity than mere words can achieve, and this encourages such groups to make a nuisance of themselves so as to attract attention. The effectiveness of such tactics depends not only on the determination of the pressure group but on the strength of the resistance that they face. If the authority whose policy they oppose is sufficiently determined, or if the public is strongly hostile to their cause, while they will achieve a great deal of publicity the only practical result of their pressure may be fines or prison terms for causing a breach of the peace. On the other hand, if the public or the authorities concerned are not committed to opposing the change which the pressure group wants, the publicity which a demonstration achieves may help to direct people's attention to the arguments of that group, or to convince them that ending the nuisance which the pressure group causes is more important than refusing to give way to them.

One aspect of the use of demonstrations to try to achieve change in the legal system that has not received consideration in the media is of considerable concern. The student of history will recall the way in which the mob was able to be used by political agitators at the time of the French Revolution. A mob is easily led, and it is no less a mob because it is involved in a demonstration. A large mob involved in a demonstration would be capable of being used by criminal groups as a cover for looting and to create the opportunity for looting. Even a peaceful demonstration requires a large police presence to control it, and this means that fewer police are available to perform their duty elsewhere. It is a mark of a free society that demonstrations can take place; but, if demonstrations become too frequent, or if they become violent, they can pose a threat to the stability of the community itself. Most demonstrators are interested in achieving a particular change, not at all in overthrowing the society in which they live. They and their leaders have to balance the desirability of the change which they are seeking against the side-effects of the methods which they are prepared to use. Furthermore, many who engage in a particular demonstration may be totally unaware of the real commitment of those organising the demonstration; alternatively, a group of activists may join a demonstration and engage in violent acts contrary to the wishes of both the organisers and of the main group of demonstrators, with the result that a legitimate cause is tarnished in the eyes of the public.

Changes in our law are not often inspired by private individuals; and, while pressure groups do play a significant role, most changes in our law come about from other causes. A great deal of the legislation today, and the vast bulk of subordinate legislation, comes about because of the policies of government departments or statutory authorities. Such bodies have an intimate knowledge of the particular field which they seek to regulate, and of the workings of the law-making machine. Such bodies are likely to have a particular Secretary of State or minister who is responsible for them before Parliament, and they naturally maintain close contact and are in an excellent position to convince the government that the legislation which they seek is desirable. They have the advantages of a pressure group, with the added advantages of status, the argument that they are acting in the public interest, and excellent contacts at the relevant level of government as well as parliamentary acceptance of their position coupled with what is by no means the least important factor – their knowledge of the processes involved and the best way of using them. An ordinary pressure group has to convince the government that the changes it is seeking are an improvement over the existing law; it is expected of a government department that it will propose subordinate legislation from time to time, and there is therefore likely to be less opposition to any particular piece of subordinate legislation which it proposes. This is also true when it seeks an Act of Parliament.

Another very powerful group bringing about changes in the legal system is made up of the local government authorities. In assessing their likely impact, it is relevant that voting to elect members of a local government authority is in most instances voting on party lines.

Political parties are able to wield greater influence than any other group of comparable size, provided that they succeed in getting a large number of their candidates elected to Parliament. They can also achieve this power if, although they have few members of Parliament, those members hold the balance of power. The active members of even the largest political parties are a very small proportion of the community as a whole, and those members who play a leading role in determining party policy are a much smaller group still; but that small group has a chance to obtain control of Parliament itself and can then bring in legislation to achieve its goals. Legislation once put into force may be difficult to reverse when a different party comes into power. One factor in this regard is that it is much easier to set up a new government department than to get rid of it if a new government sees it as no longer necessary.

The judges, by the very nature of their position, are able to achieve important changes in the law. Even when judges have no desire to change the law, as cases are heard before them they must decide in one way or the other; and their judgments will have the effect of either expanding or restricting the law in the particular field with which they are then dealing. Judges cannot avoid having some effect on the development of the law, even if they actively wish to avoid making any major change. The judges are dealing with particular cases and therefore are in constant contact with the realities of life rather than simply with broad general principles or policies. They are concerned with the law as it operates in practice. They are in a much better position to achieve small reforms in particular cases than Parliament could ever be.

Other reforms may be beyond the scope available to the judges through the processes of the development of the common law. Nevertheless, they may see the need for reform and feel compelled to draw attention to that need. Although not frequently, it does happen from time to time that a judge in such circumstances specifically records in the reasons for judgment the need that he or she sees, and sometimes the way in which he or she believes that need should be met. In some instances a judge in reasons for judgment will address remarks specifically to the Secretary of State or minister or to Parliament. When a judge does take such a step, legislation to cure the problem to which attention has been drawn may result, but unfortunately often does not.

Another means of obtaining change within the legal system is the constituting of a royal commission, a board, or a commission of enquiry. This has been used freely. In some instances the enquiries are conducted by parliamentary committees and in other instances they are conducted by persons appointed by Parliament or by the government of the day. The resultant reports can lead to important changes in the law. The effectiveness of such enquiries is, however, limited by the fact that they are enquiries into specific aspects of the law and there is certainly no guarantee that their recommendations will be accepted or will be implemented in the form that they propose or intend.

PART 2

HOW TO UNDERSTAND LEGAL AID

CHAPTER 26

LEGAL AID

What legal aid is

The definition of legal aid in the Legal Aid Handbook is:

> a system of government funding for those who cannot afford to pay for legal advice, assistance and representation.[1]

Types of legal aid

There are five types of legal aid.

- The first type is for legal help and assistance.[2] It is generally used to deal with initial help and assistance with legal problems.
- The second type is civil legal aid and covers representation in court and some preparation for civil actions.
- The third type is criminal legal aid. As its name suggests, it is provided for criminal offences.[3]
- The fourth type is free legal advice given at magistrates' courts[4] and police stations under the duty solicitor arrangements.
- There is also a fifth category of legal aid which can be granted at the discretion of the court for representation in some contempt proceedings.

The Legal Aid Board

In England and Wales[5] the Legal Aid Board has responsibility for the majority of legal aid matters. Matters are dealt with by area offices which are run by area managers and committees composed of practising solicitors and barristers who also decide on applications for civil legal aid.

Informative brochures

The Legal Aid Board publishes a series of explanatory brochures which explain how each system works.[6] Additionally, the Law Society has published a paper

---

1   *The Legal Aid Handbook* 1994, prepared by the Legal Aid Board.

2   Also known as the Green Form scheme. See the Legal Aid Act 1988 and the Legal Aid Advice and Assistance (Scope) Regulations 1989 (SI 1989/550).

3   Representation in court for criminal offences is normally financed by a Legal Aid Order. See Pt V Legal Aid Act 1988 and the Legal Aid in Criminal and Care Proceedings (General) Regulations 1989 (SI 1989/344).

4   Section 19 Legal Aid Act 1988.

5   Several other countries have similar schemes to that which exists in England and Wales although often not as comprehensive. Information about legal aid abroad is available from the Legal Department, Legal Aid Head Office, 85 Gray's Inn Road, London WC1X 8AA.

6   'How to get free or low cost legal help', 'A practical guide to Legal Aid', 'What to do if you get a summons or are questioned by the Police'.

on civil litigation and group actions which deals with the issue of funding civil actions and legal aid.[7]

The financial criteria test

Applicants for civil legal aid should be aware that they must satisfy financial criteria as well as having to convince the Legal Aid Board of the merits of their action before funding will be given.

In order to satisfy the means test for legal aid both the disposable income and capital of the applicant are taken into account.

Applications for European legal aid

Application for legal aid may be made at any time by a party who is wholly or in part unable to meet the costs of proceedings in the European Court of Justice.[8] In making an application, the applicant should set out evidence of his or her need of assistance and produce evidence from a competent authority certifying lack of means.[9] A Chamber of the European Court of Justice decides whether legal aid should be granted in full or in part, or should be refused. There is no appeal from a refusal. If circumstances change the Chamber may review the continuance of legal aid. The Court of Justice orders that a lawyer be appointed to act for the legally aided party and adjudicates on the lawyer's disbursements and fees. The court has power (in certain circumstances) to grant legal aid for the purpose of facilitating the representation or attendance of the party *on a reference to it* by a National Court or Tribunal, but the amount of money available is limited and is fixed by reference to the national currency of the State concerned.

Proposed change to the system

Less than a week before the final pages of this book were printed the Labour party (which presently comprises the ruling party in Parliament), held its annual conference. At that conference the relevant Minister stated that the legal aid system will be abolished and what is known as the contingent fee system will be expanded to replace it. That statement may or may not become law: that is for Parliament to decide. Until then this part on legal aid remains a correct explanation of the ruling law.

---

7 'Group Actions Made Easier', a report by the Law Society's Civil Litigation Committee, September 1995.

8 Rules of Procedure of the Court of Justice 1991, Article 76(1), first paragraph.

9 Rules of Procedure of the Court of Justice 1991, Article 104(3).

PART 3

HOW TO UNDERSTAND THE IMPACT OF ASPECTS OF THE EUROPEAN COMMUNITY LEGAL SYSTEM ON OUR ENGLISH LEGAL SYSTEM

CHAPTER 27

THE DIFFERENT BASES OF BRITISH AND OF EUROPEAN COMMUNITY LEGAL SYSTEMS

Court systems

In order to understand European Community law and its impact on British law it is important to appreciate that these systems of law are separate and distinct. The common law that is basic to the British legal system has no counterpart in the European Community system.

The flexibility of British law is not part of European Community law. That flexibility allows British judges to interpret British law so that it is not in conflict with European Community law. However, if a reference to the European Court of Justice is unavoidable, an interpretation of a provision of Community law given by the European Court by way of a preliminary ruling binds the British Court that made the referral.[1]

The function of a British judge and that of a European Court of Justice judge are different.

It is only in recent times that the European courts have started to build up case law.

In the hearing of prosecutions the British system is what is known as the adversary system. By contrast the approach adopted in European Community law is inquisitorial, the judge being the inquisitor.

Under the inquisitorial system judicial predilections play a greater role than under the adversary system.[2]

Treaties as the basis of European Community law

European Community law is a treaty-based law. The powers conferred by the treaties are quite wide and the Community institutions concerned with law-making have had little difficulty in promoting laws to achieve objects in respect of which there is unanimous agreement. For example, the original Treaty of Rome contained no mention of the environment; following the important Stockholm Declaration of UNCHE in 1972 a meeting was held in Paris and the then parties to the European Economic Community decided to adopt a number of environmental programmes to which a legislative effect would be given using the sweep up Article 235. With one or two exceptions, such as the inability to cope with the onset of BSE (Bovine Spongiform Encephalopathy, sometimes known as Mad Cow Disease), the environmental legislative

---

1 Case 29/68 *Milch-, Fett- und Eirkontor GmbH v Hauptzollamt Saarbrüken* [1969] ECR 165 at 179 and following.

2 The advantages and disadvantages of the adversarial and inquisitorial systems are considered in Chapter 14.

programme has been a great success in achieving objectives although originally having Article 235 as a legal basis. This was corrected by the European Single Act and developed under the Treaty on European Union. Thus the treaties provide a legal basis upon which to found secondary legislation consisting of regulations and decisions with immediate legally binding effect and directives indicating to Member States how they are to enact national legislation to achieve uniform Community objectives. A body of case law is, however, being built up by the European Court of Justice which has established a body of rules for the interpretation of Community law.

Thus European Community law consists of various treaties, Acts of Accession, regulations, decisions, directives, and rights, liabilities, obligations and restrictions from time to time arising by or under the treaties and all remedies and procedures from time to time provided for, by or under the treaties as in accordance with the treaties are without further enactment to be given legal effect or used in Britain.

British law is based upon Acts of Parliament and statutory instruments giving detailed effect to that law, and common law as declared by the judges over a long period of time together with certain laws stemming from the exercise of the Royal prerogative. Treaties do not have immediate binding effect in British law. The provisions of treaties have to be brought into effect by statute or orders in Council, although under the European Communities Act European Community regulations have a directly binding effect and it has recently become accepted practice for provisions of international conventions to be directly applied by European Community regulations. For example, Article 32 of Council Regulation EC 259/93 provides that the provisions of the international transport conventions listed in Annex 1 to the regulation to which Member States are parties shall be complied with insofar as they cover the subject of waste to which the regulation refers. Those conventions as listed include ADR, COTIF, RID, SOLAS, CHICAGO, MARPOL and ADNR. At international level European law is therefore becoming much more integrated than hitherto.

Subordinate legislation

Subordinate legislation in the European Union takes the form of regulations, decisions and directives. Regulations and decisions are immediately binding on coming into force. Directives are addressed to Member States, requiring them to bring in appropriate legislation within the time-scale laid down. If this is exceeded, certain provisions of directives may then have direct effect. These are provisions which are mandatory in nature, clear and precise, unconditional and leaving no discretion to the Member State as regards implementation.

The incoming tide of European Community law has 'filled our rivers and estuaries and nothing can hold it back'.[3]

---

3   *HP Bulmer Limited v J Bollinger SA* [1974] 401 at 418, 419; [1974] 2 All ER 1226 at 1231, 1232; [1974] 2 CMLR 91 at 111, 112 Lord Denning MR in the English Court of Appeal.

Points of conflict

Part I of the European Communities Act 1972 contains general provisions enabling European Community law to be incorporated at one stroke in the English legal system, in accordance with the Community treaties and the Act of Accession 1972, and to be given precedence over conflicting prior English law. Enforceable Community rights are received including the jurisprudence of the European Community Courts of which the doctrine of supremacy forms an integral part.

English law allows custom over a sufficient length of time to provide a basis for an English court's decision, but provisions of European Community law are not to be interpreted in the light of custom unless there is an express reference to allow custom to be used.[4]

There may be disputes over legislation or subordinate legislation made by the European Community but which introduces factors that are not acceptable to the United Kingdom. Disputes may also be involved (and are likely to arise increasingly in the future) over directives issued by the European Community. Those disputes must be decided upon, not by the English, Scottish or Northern Irish judges, but by the European Court – a court which, as we have seen, does not have a doctrine of precedent, leaving each case to be decided without that important benefit.

---

4   Case 12/73 *Muras v Hauptzollamt Hamburg-Jonas* [1973] ECR 963 at 974.

CHAPTER 28

THE BASIC TREATIES

The Basic European Community Treaties

There are three basic European treaties namely the Treaty of Rome which set up the original European Economic Community, the Treaty of Paris which set up the European Coal and Steel Community and the Euratom Treaty which established the European Atomic Energy Community. These treaties and various Acts of Accession with their protocols together with the Treaty on European Union comprise the basic European law which must be read together with certain conventions and Council Decisions.

The Treaty of Rome

The Treaty of Rome has been amended a number of times, perhaps most significantly by the Single European Act and the Treaty on European Union. The European Economic Community was renamed the European Community and the Act was renamed the Treaty establishing the European Community. It consists of six parts, the first dealing with principles, the second with citizenship of the Union, the third with Community policies, the fourth with association of the overseas countries and territories, the fifth with Community institutions and the sixth with the setting up of the institutions and with final provisions.

Treaty-based policies

Community policies are now grouped under 17 titles dealing with the free movement of goods, agriculture, the free movement of persons, services and capital, transport, common laws on competition, taxation and approximation of laws, economic and monetary policy, a common commercial policy, social policy, education, vocational training and youth, culture, public health, consumer protection, Trans-European Networks, industry, economic and social cohesion, research and technological development, environment and development co-operation.[1]

European Community economic policies – coal and steel

The European Coal and Steel Community has as its task to contribute, in harmony with the general economy of the Member States and through the establishment of a common market, to economic expansion, growth, employment and a rising standard of living in the Member States. The four institutions of the Community, being the High Authority, the European Parliament, the Council and the Court must, among other matters, within the

---

1   The Treaty as amended is reproduced (except for the Preamble and Annexes) in Vaughan, Law of The European Communities Service, Butterworths, London.

limits of their respective powers, in the common interest, ensure an orderly supply of coal and steel to the common market, ensure that all consumers have equal access to the sources of production and ensure the maintenance of conditions which will encourage undertakings to expand and improve their production potential and to promote a policy of using natural resources rationally and avoiding their unconsidered exhaustion. Economic and social provisions are set out in Title 3 to the Treaty under 10 chapter headings covering such matters as finance, production, prices, agreements and concentrations, transport, wages and movement of workers and commercial policy.

European Community nuclear policy

The Treaty establishing the European Atomic Energy Community sets out in Article 1 the task of the Community to contribute to the raising of the standard of living in the Member States and the development of relations with other countries by creating the conditions necessary for the speedy establishment and growth of nuclear industries. Article 3 provides that the tasks shall be carried out by four institutions, namely a European Parliament, a Council, a Commission and a Court of Justice. In order to perform its task Euratom must promote research and ensure dissemination of technical information; establish uniform safety standards to protect the health of workers and of the general public and ensure that they are applied; facilitate investment and ensure, particularly by encouraging ventures on the part of undertakings, the establishment of the basic installations necessary for the development of nuclear energy in the Community; ensure that all users in the Community receive a regular and equitable supply of all the nuclear fuels; make certain by appropriate supervision, that nuclear materials are not diverted to purposes other than those for which they are intended; exercise the right of ownership conferred upon it with respect to special fissile materials; ensure wide commercial outlets and access to the best technical facilities by the creation of a common market in specialised materials and equipment, by the free movement of capital for investment in the field of nuclear energy and by freedom of employment for specialists within the Community; and establish with other countries and international organisations such relations as will foster progress in the peaceful uses of nuclear energy.

Title 2 sets out provisions for encouragement of progress in the field of nuclear energy under 10 chapter headings covering, *inter alia*, the promotion of research, the dissemination of information, health and safety, investment, joint undertakings, supplies, safeguards, proper ownership in the nuclear common market and external relations.

CHAPTER 29

EUROPEAN COMMUNITY INSTITUTIONS

Mergers under the Treaty of Rome

The merger of the institutions serving the three Communities which had been set up was achieved in two stages on the same day as the two Treaties of Rome were signed (setting up the then EEC and Euratom). A convention on certain institutions common to the European Communities was signed providing for a single European Parliament and a single Court of Justice to serve all three Communities. In 1965 a treaty establishing a single Council and a single Commission of the European Communities (the Merger Treaty) was signed amending the treaties resulting in a Community consisting of three separate legal entities being served by common institutions. Thus there is only one Council, albeit functioning in different specialisations, and one Commission. In addition, it created a Committee of permanent representatives of the Member States (COREPER) and charged it with responsibility for preparing the work of the Council and for carrying out the tasks assigned to it by the Council. A unified civil service of the Communities was created from persons employed separately by each Community. The civil service is now governed by uniform staff regulations and conditions of employment. The Single European Act 1986 in effect converted the summit meetings of the heads of State or of government of the Member States into an effective European Council and authorised the setting up of a court of first instance. It also enhanced the status of the European Parliament which became more involved in the decision-making process of the Communities as a result.

The Community institutions

The Community institutions are the European Council, the European Parliament, the European Commission, the Court of Auditors, the Court of Justice and various subsidiary institutions such as consultative bodies, management and rule-making committees, the European Investment Bank and institutions of monetary union all supported by the European Bank for Reconstruction and Development. Their authority stems from the founding treaties which impose upon the institutions certain tasks. The main institutions are empowered by the founding treaties to take decisions and make rules which can be directly and immediately binding not only upon Member States but also upon the citizens of Member States. There is no separation of powers between the legislative and the executive function. The judicial function is, however, separate subject to certain quasi-judicial powers which the European Commission has of a limited nature.

The impact of European Community institutions on British law

British governmental policy to enact a particular statute may find its origin, not in a policy of the Cabinet or the Party room, but in the policy of one of the organs of the European Community.

The Council of the European Community Union

The Council of the European Union consists of representatives of the 15 Member States. The Ministers of Foreign Affairs attend monthly Council meetings known as General Council meetings dealing with political matters. The Ministers of Economic Affairs and Finance attend on a regular basis another kind of General Council meeting called ECOFIN which oversees the working of the internal market and of legislation in economic and financial affairs. Other Council meetings can be of a specialist nature, such as the Environment Ministers meeting together or Agriculture Ministers meeting together or Transport Ministers meeting together. Sometimes there are joint meetings where there is an overlap between the specialist portfolios. The Council is the main decision-making body, the coordinating body and the principal legislative body although some legislation is promoted jointly between the Council and the Parliament.

Community actions have to be based on specific treaty provisions; implied powers will not suffice. In the case of the Council, in 1987 a Council Regulation on generalised tariff preferences was challenged by the Commission on the ground that it was incorrect to rely on Article 235 of the Treaty because Article 113 was the correct legal basis. The European Court of Justice found in favour of the Commission.[1]

The importance of relying on specific treaty provisions lies in the voting procedure laid down. There are three different voting requirements for the Council, namely unanimity, simple majority and qualified majority. Unanimity is required for the most important matters such as constitutional measures. Unless otherwise provided for in the Treaties the Council must act by a majority of its members. Curiously, very few matters are governed by a simple majority. A weighted voting system enables decisions to be taken by a qualified majority. France, Germany, Italy and the United Kingdom have 10 votes each, Spain has eight, Belgium, Greece, The Netherlands and Portugal have five each, Austria and Sweden have four each, Denmark, Finland and Ireland have three each and Luxembourg has two. Where a Council Decision is required to be taken upon a proposal from the Commission a qualified majority of any 62 out of the total of 87 votes will suffice but there are certain complications under an agreement reached at an extraordinary Council meeting held in Luxembourg on the 29 January 1966 (the so called Accords of Luxembourg). Where a decision is to be reached by the qualified majority procedure on a proposal emanating from the Commission, the Council should endeavour to reach such a decision

---

1   Case 45/86 *Commission v Council* [1987] ECR 1493.

unanimously whenever the vital interests of one or more of the Member States are involved. The Council functions within the framework of the Treaties according to its own rules of procedure. It has a president. This office rotates amongst the Member States for terms of six months commencing 1 January and 1 July in every year in a pre-determined order. The president draws up the provisional agenda for each meeting.

The European Parliament

The European Parliament consists of elected representatives from Member States, the first direct elections having been held in 1979 in accordance with national electoral procedures in each Member State. The allocation of seats broadly reflects population distribution in the Community. Members are elected for five years. It has determined its own method of working being relatively free of restriction under the founding Treaties which contain only a few guidelines for the organisation and work of Parliament. It functions through its political groups and standing committees. After the 1994 elections there were 10 political groups. The European Parliament has 20 standing committees each specialising in a particular area of Community policy. The committees draw up reports which form the basis of debates. The Treaty on European Union provides that the Court of Justice has jurisdiction to review the legality of Acts adopted jointly by the European Parliament and the Council and of Acts of the European Parliament intended to produce legal effects so far as the parties are concerned.[2]

Originally the European Parliament was merely a consultative and advisory body. Following the Maastricht Treaty it participates in decision-making in accordance with a highly complex set of procedures. Under certain treaty articles Parliament has to be consulted in the legislative process. In other cases it does not have to be consulted. The treaties do not spell out what is involved in consultation. Where a consultation is mandatory the Commission in promoting legislation has to follow Parliament's opinion. In certain cases where the Council intends to disregard Parliament's opinion, under a joint declaration of the European Parliament and the Council and the Commission of the 4 March 1975, the matter has to be referred to a conciliation committee.

There are three different kinds of procedures of promoting Community legislation involving the Parliament known as the consultation procedure, co-operation procedure and the co-decision procedure. In the consultation procedure the Commission forwards a proposal for a regulation or directive to the Council which refers it to Parliament and to the Economic and Social Committee. When the opinions are received by the Commission it can amend its proposal and refer an amended proposal to the Council. In the co-operation procedure the Commission sends its proposal to the Council which passes it to Parliament and to the Economic and Social Committee. The Council then has to adopt a common position on the proposal in the light of the opinions received. The common position is sent to Parliament which has three months to accept,

2   EC Treaty Article 173 as amended by Article G53 of the Treaty on European Union.

reject or propose amendments to it on its second reading. Parliament decides by an absolute majority of its component members. The Commission then, within one month, re-examines the proposal which goes back to the Council together with the Commission's opinion on the amendments of Parliament not accepted. The Council can adopt Parliament's amendments unanimously. It can adopt the Commission's re-examined proposal by a qualified majority. It can amend the Commission's re-examined proposal unanimously. If the Council does not decide within three months, the proposal is deemed not to have been accepted. The co-decision procedure follows the co-operation procedure save that it introduces a conciliation committee to resolve conflicts between Parliament and Council. It is important in each case to examine the precise requirements of the article or articles of the treaty under which a proposal is being promoted because the procedures are so complicated.

The European Commission

The European Commission exercises the exclusive right of initiating legislation. Its president and members are appointed for a period of five years. Their appointments are renewable. At the present time it has 20 members. Two come from France, Germany, Italy, Spain and the United Kingdom and the remaining countries provide one commissioner each. Each commissioner is assisted by a group of civil servants known as a Cabinet. The Commission is divided into 22 specialist directorates-general which in turn are divided into directorates and directorates are divided into divisions. The commissioners are supported by a secretariat, a legal service, an interpretation service, a statistical office and the customs union service.

The Commission is a kind of enforcement agency. It has to ensure that Community law is complied with. It checks to see whether Member States have properly implemented directives into their national law. It carries out certain monitoring functions. It collects data. It is an active participator in Community activities along with the Council and the European Parliament.

The Court of Auditors

The Court of Auditors presently consists of 15 members holding office for renewable terms of six years. The Court, located in Luxembourg, looks at the legalities and regularity of the Community accounts and the revenue and expenditure of all bodies set up by the Community. It presents an annual report which is published together with the replies of the institutions to the observations made in the report in the *Official Journal*.

The European Court of Justice

The European Court of Justice is comprised of the European Court and the Court of First Instance. The European Court at present has 15 judges and 9 Advocates General. Each Member State is thus represented by a judge. The European Court of Justice has appellate jurisdiction over the Court of First Instance. The Court of First Instance has 15 judges but no Advocates General.

CHAPTER 30

THE EFFECT OF THE EUROPEAN COMMUNITY LEGAL SYSTEM ON BRITAIN

Effect on the British Parliament

Regulations and decisions made within the European Community legal system have immediate binding effect on the day they come into force. Some of these may have been voted through under the qualified majority voting system. If Britain uses its 10 votes to vote against a proposal the proponents for a measure require 62 votes out of the remaining 77. The British Parliament is therefore no longer supreme in respect of that area of law-making. Directives are required to be implemented by Member States in their national legislation within the time stipulated. Whilst the form of some directives gives the British Parliament enormous scope to be interpretative of the Community's intention, the Commission has the responsibility of checking whether or not Britain has in its view properly implemented legislation. If it feels that it has not it brings an Article 169 proceeding against the British government and issues a reasoned opinion. The matter is then determined by the European Court which can rule that Britain is at fault in not complying with Community law.

Provision of directives which are clear and precise and leave no discretion to Member States as to how the matter is to be implemented and are in mandatory format will have direct effect notwithstanding that they have not been implemented within the time laid down by the directive for implementation under the so-called doctrine of 'direct effect'. There are also procedures designed to inhibit the British Parliament's ability to introduce new laws where the Community is proposing to legislate on the same subject.

A great deal of parliamentary time is now taken up by the promotion of secondary legislation to bring into force a whole range of Community directives. If Parliament enacts statutes which are inconsistent with Community law there is a risk of the European Court of Justice declaring such law void which could lead to claims for compensation as in the case of the Spanish fishermen.

Effect on the British courts

The supremacy of European Community law has been recognised unanimously by the House of Lords.[1] To ensure that British law is consistent with Community law some judges have been in the habit of interpreting British legislation in such a way as to ensure that it does accord with Community law. This is because the British courts are under a duty to give a purposive construction to the regulations in a manner which would accord with the decisions of the European Court of Justice on the directive. Where necessary, words can be implied which would achieve that effect. So the House of Lords implied into Regulation 5(3) after the words 'immediately before the transfer'

---

1   *R v Darby* [1980] 2 All ER 166; [1980] 2 WLR 597; [1980] 2 CMLR 229. See further Emma Chown, 'The Undeniable Supremacy of EC Law', *NLJ*, 12.3.93, pp 337–38.

the words 'or would have been so implied if he had not been unfairly dismissed in the circumstances described by Regulation 8(1)' in the British case of *Litster v Forth Dry Dock & Engineering Company Limited*.[2]

In another case the House of Lords held that the purpose for which s 1(2)(c) Equal Pay Act 1970 was enacted was to implement Britain's obligations of equal pay under Article 119 of the EEC Treaty and Council Directive EEC 75/1177. Accordingly, if a female employee was employed on work of equal value to the work of a man doing another job for the employer, she was entitled under s 1(2)(c) to claim equal pay with that man notwithstanding that there was another man doing the same work as her for the same pay.[3]

Where points of Community law crop up the British courts should refer these points to the European Court of Justice for a decision before coming to a conclusion in the matter. Thus, for example, the House of Lords in the case of *R v Secretary of State for the Environment ex p The Royal Society for the Protection of Birds* referred two questions to the European Court of Justice on 9 February 1995 namely:

1. Is a Member State entitled to take account of the considerations mentioned in Article 2 of Directive 79/409/EEC of 2 April 1979 on the conservation of wild birds (the Birds Directive) when classifying an area as a special protection area and/or in defining the boundaries of such an area pursuant to Article 4(1) and/or Article 4(2) of that directive?

2. If the answer to the question is no, may a Member State nevertheless take account of Article 2 considerations in the classification process insofar as:

    (a) they amount to a general interest which is superior to a general interest which is represented by the ecological objective of the directive;

    (b) they amount to imperative reasons of overriding public interest such as might be taken into account under Article 6(4) of Directive 92/43 EEC of 21 May 1992 on the conservation of natural habitats and wild fauna and flora?

This case is interesting because it shows the slightly insular approach adopted in Britain. The promoters of the use of Lappel Bank for commercial purposes appear to have wanted to tackle the matter through attacking the classification. *The Santona Marshes case*[4] had already shown how strict an interpretation of the Birds Directive would be likely to be applied by the European Court. Amongst the 100 different species of birds living in the Santona Marshes is the spoonbill which features in Annex 1 of the Birds Directive. It was alleged that by not classifying the Marshes as an SPA, Spain was in breach of Articles 41 and 42 of the Directive. The courts held that whilst Member States retained a certain degree of discretion in respect of the choice of SPAs the classification of areas nonetheless had to be based on ecological criteria determined by the Directive. The classification of the Marshes as a nature reserve did not satisfy the

---

2   [1990] AC 546, HL.

3   *Pickstone v Freemans plc* [1989] AC 66, HL.

4   Case C-355/90 *Commission v Spain* [1993] 1 ECR 4221.

Directive's requirements both in view of territorial scope as well as status. Spain had therefore failed in its obligations, particularly those under Article 4(4).

Contrast this approach with the German approach. The authorities in Germany wanted to construct the A20 motorway across the Peene Valley which would interrupt breeding and nesting places for a considerable number of rare, endangered birds and would destroy a certain amount of bog woodland and residual forest, both being priority habitat types under the Habitats Directive. The Commission's opinion was applied for and given on the 18 December 1995 allowing the motorway to be constructed because Article 6(4) Habitats Directive in effect allows a derogation from the general obligation to maintain the integrity of a special area of conservation when a project must be carried out for imperative reasons of overriding public interest including those of a social and economic nature. Where the site concerns, as in this case, a priority natural habitat type and/or a priority species, it is possible, further to an opinion from the Commission, to carry out works for imperative reasons of overriding public interest. In this case the Commission held that the high level of unemployment in Mecklenburgh-Western Pomerania was an imperative reason of overriding public interest. Whether the Commission would come to the same conclusion so far as employment in the vicinity of the port of Sheerness is concerned may perhaps be questionable. In the event the European Court of Justice on 11 July 1996 found against the Port of Sheerness and held that a Member State may take account of a general interest which is superior to the general interest which is represented by an ecological object of a directive (subject to any inherent obligation to take compensatory measures) but that economic requirements do not constitute a superior general interest for these purposes. The Court held secondly that a Member State may not take into account economic requirements which it considers may amount to imperative reasons for overriding public interest within the meaning of Article 6(4) Directive 92/43.

Article 177 EC Treaty provides that the Court of Justice should have jurisdiction to give preliminary rulings concerning the interpretation of the EC Treaty, the validity and interpretation of acts of the institutions of the Community and the interpretation of the statutes of bodies established by an act of the Council where those statutes so provide. Where such a question is raised before any court or Tribunal for a Member State, that court or Tribunal may, if it considers that a decision on the question is necessary to enable it to give judgment, request the Court of Justice to give a ruling thereon. Where any such question is raised in a case pending before a court or Tribunal of a Member State against whose decisions there is no judicial remedy under national law, that court or Tribunal must bring the matter before the Court of Justice. Hence the Court has been asked to interpret the meaning of emergencies and limited period of time in Article 10(10) Directive 80/77 relating to the quality of water intended for human consumption,[5] the meaning of individual concern in Article 146 Euratom Treaty[6] and the meaning of waste included in Directives 75/442 on

---

5   Case 228/87 *Pretura Unificata di Torino v Persons Unknown* [1988] ECR 5099.

6   Case T-219/95R *Danielsson and Others v Commission* (unreported).

waste and 78/319 on toxic and dangerous wastes.[7] The meaning of the word 'waste' in Community law is a very vexed subject, to such an extent that, when implementing the latest waste directive, the British regulations, instead of attempting to define the meaning of waste in British law, simply legislated that waste should mean whatever waste meant in Community law. This kind of approach will undoubtedly inhibit the British judiciary in the way that the litigation is dealt with involving construction of the Waste Regulations. It does, however, provide an interesting example.

---

7   Case C-359/88 E *Zanetti and Others* [1990] ECR 1509.

CHAPTER 31

NOW READ ON

Further reading

The object of the present book is to set out as simply as possible the nature and workings of the English legal system. The footnotes in this book have given references to cases in which the workings of the system have been clarified by the judges.

It is important to bear in mind that this book is one of a developing series. Other books in the series are important to a fuller understanding of the English system. It is no accident that the first in this series of books in plain English is a statement in plain words of the basic rules the courts use in interpreting statutes, subordinate legislation, and many other categories of documents.

Textbook on the English system

Gifford, Dr DJ, PhD (Cantab) and Salter, John R, MA (Oxon), *How to Understand an Act of Parliament*, 1996, Cavendish Publishing Limited, London.

Textbooks on the European Community system

Vaughan (ed), *Law of the European Communities Service*, 1996, Butterworths, London.

Salter, John R, MA (Oxon), *European Environmental Law*, 1996, Kluwer Law International, London.

INDEX

Absurdity in legislation, 28

Acts of Parliament
  See Statute law

Adjournment, 92–93

Admissions, 60, 77

Adversary system, 69–71

Advantages, 69–70
  disadvantages, 70–71
  ethics, 69
  evidence, 70
  judges, 87
  legal profession, excluding, 71
  meaning, 69

Affidavits, 57

Affirmation, 57, 60

Affirming decisions, 40

Amendments
  delegated legislation, 34
  statutes, 12, 19, 27–28

Appeals, 112, 113

Appearance, 57

Approving decisions, 41

Arbitration, 53, 123–24

Backbenchers, 20, 103

Bail, 65–66, 111

Bar, 49–50

Barristers, 49, 50, 67

Bias
  See Impartiality

Bills, 18, 21–22

Blasphemy, 86

Bonds, 92

Burden of proof, 79

Cabinet, 13–14, 17, 21

Capital punishment, 88

Certainty, importance of, 38–39, 98–99

Certiorari, 56, 113–14

Change and the law, 43, 46, 127–31
  common law, 127, 131

crime, 127
demonstrations, 128, 129
effectiveness of changing, 128–31
European Union, 127
Government, 131
judges, 131
lobbying, 17, 129
local government, 131
pressure groups, 128, 129–30
representations, 128–29
subordinate legislation, 130

Children
  criminal capacity, 63
  juvenile offenders, 93
  press, 93
  punishment, 3, 87–88, 91, 93
  Youth Training Centres, 91

Civil cases
  damages, 55, 58
  decisions, 55–56, 61
  delay, 111
  discover, 58
  enforcement, 61–62
  hearings, 59–61
  interlocutory proceedings, 59
  interrogatories, 58
  juries, 79, 80, 81
  jurisdiction, 54–56
  legal representation, 59
  locus standi, 55
  pleadings, 57–58
  standard of proof, 61
  trials of, 57–62

Commission, 145, 147, 148

Committees, 14, 18, 106

Common law, 5–8
  change and the law, 127
  courts, 5–7, 46
  custom, 10
  effectiveness, 8, 46
  finding, 6–7, 11–12
  flexibility, 7
  limitations, 115–17
  overriding by Parliament, 9
  principles as constituting, 5, 42
  status of court vital, 5
  statute law affecting, 115–16
  textbooks, 6–7

Compensation
See Damages

Compromise, 54, 99

Conciliation, 53

Consumer protection, 87, 116

Contempt of court, 61–62

Corporal punishment, 91

Corporations, 59, 67

Costs, 54, 56, 110

Counterclaims, 58

Courts
See also Judges
commencement of proceedings, 54
common law, 5–7, 46
county courts, 6, 54
Court of Appeal, 6, 39, 43
Court of Session, 39
delay, 53, 111–13
European Court of Justice, 42, 52, 136, 140, 141, 145, 148–49
European Union, effect on, 149–50
excluding, 123–24
hierarchy, 5–6, 37, 38, 40, 41, 54
High Court, 6
House of Lords, 6, 39
jurisdiction, 54–56
lack of preparedness, 110
law-making, 46
limitations, 109–14
Press in, 65, 93
superior, 6, 9, 11, 38, 57
tribunals, 6, 37, 42, 54, 123
unavailability, 113–14

Crime, 120, 127

Criminal cases, 63–68
See also Punishment, Sentencing
bail, 65–66
children, 63
declarations, 96–97
double jeopardy, 66
evidence, 64
facts and law, 68
fair trials, 65, 80, 81

insanity, 63, 89–90
intention, 63
interrogations, 64–65
investigation, 64
juries, 79–82
jurisdiction, 54–55
legal representation, 67
miscarriages of justice, 74
penalties, 47, 87
pleas, 65
previous convictions, 67, 74–75
remand, 65–66, 111
right to prosecute, 65
right to silence, 64–65
strict liability, 63–64
summary trials, 66
trials of, 66, 67–68

Cross-examination, 60, 71

Crown, 14–15, 120

Custom, 10, 12, 141

Damages
case study, 4–5
civil law, 55, 58
delay, 112
head injuries, 5–7
juries, 79, 81
personal injuries, 4–7
psychiatric harm, 4–5

Death penalty, 88

Decisions, 140

Declarations, 56, 96–97

Default judgments, 57

Defence, 57–58, 59

Definitions overlooked
in statutes, 27

Delay, 53, 98–99, 111–13

Delegated legislation
See Subordinate legislation

Demonstrations, 128–29

Departments of government
See Government departments

Detection, 120

Deterrence, 87, 89

Directives, 15, 52, 86, 140, 149–51

Disapproving of decisions, 41

Discovery, 58, 59

Disputes
abandoning, 53
arbitration, 53
commencement of proceedings, 54
conciliation, 53
costs, 54
courts, 54–56
disposing of disputes
without courts, 52–54
Government, with, 51, 52
handling within the
legal system, 51–56
individuals, between, 51
judges, 54
jurisdiction, 54
magistrates, 54
mediation, 53
self-help, 52–53, 86
settlement, 54, 110
State, with, 51

Distinguishing decisions, 41

Distress, 61

Documentary evidence, 60, 73

Double jeopardy, 66

Elections, 102, 104–05

Employment, 42, 52

Enforcement of law, 4, 95, 109
See also Prosecution
and punishment
civil decisions, 61–62
community acceptance, lack of, 119
contempt of court, 61–62
detection of crime, 120
distress, 61
enforceability distinguished, 4
European union, 148
Government, 120–21
limitations on, 119–21
police, 95
self-help, 52–53, 86
undertakings, 62

Environmental protection, 43, 121, 139–40
European Commission, 145, 147, 148
European Council, 145, 146–47
European Court of Justice, 42, 52, 136, 140, 141, 145, 148–49
European Parliament, 145, 147–48
European Union, 8, 139–51
change and the law, 127
conflicts, 139, 141
COREPER, 145
courts, effect on, 149–50
custom, 141
decisions, 140
direct effect, 149
directives, 15, 52, 86, 140, 149–51
disputes, 52
environmental protection, 139–40
European Coal and
Steel Community, 143–44
European Court of Justice, 42, 52, 136, 140, 141, 145, 148–49
institutions, 139, 145–48
judges, 139
law, impact of, on, 146
legal aid, 136
legal system, impact on, 149–52
legality of acts, 147
legislation, 147–48
MEPs, 147
mergers, 145
nuclear policy, 144
Parliament, effect on, 149
policy, 17
precedence of EC law, 15, 141, 149
preliminary rulings, 139, 151–52
regulations, 140
statute law, 140
subordinate legislation, 140
treaties, 139–40, 143–46
voting, 146–47, 149

Evidence
See also Witnesses
admissions, 60, 77
adversarial system, 70

circumstantial, 75
criminal cases, 64
cross-examination, 60, 71
documentary, 60, 73
evaluation, 75
experts, 60–61
hearsay, 76
improperly obtained, 64
inadmissible, 74–75
in-chief, 60, 71
interrogatories, 58
judicial notice, 76
meaning, 73
miscarriages of justice, 74
presumption of accuracy, 76
prima facie, 76
primary, 73
real, 73
re-examination, 60, 71
rules, 73–77
secondary, 73
types, 73–74
without prejudice, 77
witnesses, 60

Expenses of litigation
See Costs

Expert witnesses, 60–61

Fair trials, 65, 80, 81

Fairness, 8

Fines, 91–92

Fraud, 82

Further and better particulars, 59

Government
Cabinet, 13–14, 17, 21
departments, 17, 104, 107, 131
forming, 45
individuals suing, 51
ministers, 14, 45, 103
opposition, 19–20, 45, 103
policy, 17, 104
pressure of business, 103
privilege, 120–21
protecting itself from the law, 120–21
regulation of industry
and commerce, 125

Secretaries of State, 3, 13–14

Habeas corpus, 56, 114
Hansard, 30
Hearings
civil cases, 55–56, 59–61
decisions, 124
justices of peace, 59–60
magistrates, 59–60
procedure, 60–61
urgent, 55, 96, 113
Hearsay, 76
House of Lords, 6, 13, 20–21, 39, 102

Ignorance of law, excuse as, 109, 119
Imprisonment, 56
children, 87–88
conditions, 88–89
contempt of court, 61–62
deterrence, 89
long-term, 87–88
parole, 93
periodic, 90
psychiatric treatment during, 89–90
work release, 90
Impartiality
importance, 80
judges, 80, 98
legal profession, 54, 69, 80
Indictable offences, 66
Injunctions, 55, 59
Inquisitorial system, 70, 98, 139
Insanity, 63, 89–90
Interlocutory proceedings, 59
Interrogatories, 58, 59
Investigation of offences, 64

Judges
adversarial system, 98
conservative, 46, 97, 116–17
criminal cases, 65
developing the law, 5–7, 37–43, 46
effectiveness, 97–98

European Court of Justice, 139, 148
hierarchy, 54
impartiality, 80, 98
See Statutory interpretation
Parliament, 46
qualifications, 54
reform, 117
settlement, achieved by, 54
shortage of, 111
spare, need of, 111
statutory interpretation, 29, 95
subordinate legislation, 35
textbooks, 6–7
weaknesses in law found by, 17–18
witnesses, questioning, 60, 98

Judgments in default, 57

Judicial notice, 76

Judicial review, 114

Jurisdiction, 54–56

Juries, 79–83
bias, 80
burden of proof, 79
challenging, 67, 81
civil cases, 79, 80, 81
criminal cases, 79–81, 82
criticisms, 80–81
damages, 81
exemptions, 81, 82
extension, 81–82
fair trials, 65, 80, 81
fraud, 82
function, 79
justification, 80
magistrates' courts, 81–92
origin, 79
press, 81, 82
punishment, 87
reform, 82–83
restriction, 81–82
selection, 80–81

Justices of the Peace, 5, 37, 54, 59–60

Juvenile offenders, 93

Land disputes, 51–2

Law
binding, 39, 40
change and, 43, 46, 127–31

confidence in, 47
consistency, 47
enforcement, 4
European Institutions,
effect on, 146
finding, 6–7, 11–12
fundamental basis of
society preserved, 85
interpreting
See Statutory interpretation
limitations, 115–17
making, 3, 9,
45–47, 105–08
merchant, 10
nature, 3–4
outmoded, 18
public order preserved, 85
reports, 6, 11–12, 109
rules outside legal system, 3–4
sources, 5–10
test of, 3
unintelligible, 106
visitors bound by, 4

Lay advocates, 72

Legal aid, 67, 135–36
brochures, 135–36
European Union, 136
financial eligibility, 136
Legal Aid Board, 135
meaning, 135
reform, 136
types, 135

Legal profession
See also Judges
arbitration, 123–24
barristers, 49, 67
changing role, 123–25
civil cases, 59
criminal cases, 67
duty to the court, 69
ethics, 69, 71, 110
exclusion of, 1, 123
new fields, extension of
profession into, 124–25
objectivity, 54, 69
Queen's Counsel, 49, 50, 67
settlement achieved by, 54
solicitors, 49

specialisation,   49–50, 124
training,   110, 123
Legal standing,   55, 113
Legal system
  acceptability,   127–8
  development,   41–42
  European Union, effect of,   149–52
  human frailties,   95–98
  limitations,   95–99
  rules outside,   3–4
Legitimate expectations,   8
Licensing,   37
Life peers,   102
Limitations of the law
  common law,   115–17
  conflicting needs,   98–99
  courts,   109
  enforcement,   119
  human frailties,   95–98
  importance of knowing,   99
  inevitability, of,   95–99
  Parliament,   101–06
  subordinate law-making
    bodies,   107–08
Litigants in person,   69, 109
Lobbying,   17, 129
Local government,   17, 107, 131
Locus standi,   55, 113

Magistrates,   5, 54–55,
                                             59–60, 81–82
Making law,   3, 9
Mandamus,   56, 113
Mediation,   43
Members of Parliament,   34, 45
  choice,   101–02
  recall of,   105
Merchant law,   10
Ministers,   13–14, 45, 103
  choosing,   45
  circulars by,   30
  disputes,   52
  drafting legislation,   19
  House of Lords,   20

responsibility,   13, 34
secrecy,   120
Minority views,   102–03, 104, 105
Miscarriages of justice,   74
Murder,   63, 66, 127

Natural justice,   8
Nature of law,   3–4
Negligence,   39–40, 116
Notice of motion,   57
Nuclear policy,   144

Oaths,   57, 60
Obiter dicta,   40
Offences, investigation of,   64
Offenders, reform of,   87–88
Overruling decisions,   38, 39, 41

Parliament,   13–15
  See also Statute law,
  Subordinate legislation
  backbenchers,   20, 103
  Cabinet,   13–14, 17
  common law,   9
  committees,   14, 18, 106
  Crown,   13–15
  effectiveness limited,   45–46, 101–06
  elections,   102, 104–05
  European law, effect of,   149
  European Parliament,   145, 147–48
  Government departments,   105–06
  Houses, two,   13
  information sources,   106
  intention of,   29, 30
  judges,   46
  limitations,   101–06
  making law,   9, 17–22,
                                             45–46, 105–06
  Members of Parliament,   45, 101–04
  ministerial responsibility,   13, 34
  origins,   13, 45
  Prime Minister,   15
  purpose,   101
  Queen's Speech,   15

representations of sections
of the community, 102–03
responsiveness to changes
in electorate, 104–05
right of recall, 105
safe seats, 102
Secretaries of State, 3, 13, 14
separation of powers, 101
sovereignty, 15, 141, 149
subordinate legislation, 45–46
voting, 45

Parole, 93

Party system, 19, 45, 103

Perfection, 98–99

Periodic detention, 90

Petitions, 105

Planning, 38

Pleadings, 57–58

Pleas, 65

Police
enforcement, 95
helping the police with
their inquiries, 64–65
interrogation, 64–65
punishment, 86

Precedent, 116–17
abandoning, 42
affirming decisions, 40
approving decisions, 41
binding, 39, 40
certainty, 38–39
Court of Appeal, 39, 43
Court of Session, 39, 40
disapproving decisions, 41
distinguishing decisions, 41
doctrine of, 6, 38–43
European Court of Justice, 42, 52
House of Lords, 39
obiter dicta, 40
overruling, 38, 39, 41
persuasive, 39, 40
Privy Council, 39
restricting development
of legal system, 41–42
reversing decisions, 40

Prerogative writs, 56, 113–14

Press
children, 93
court in, 65, 93
juries, 81, 82

Pressure groups, 19, 30, 103,
106, 128–30

Presumption of innocence, 67

Previous convictions, 67, 74–75

Prime Minister, 15

Prior convictions, 67, 74–75

Prisons
See Imprisonment

Private Members' Bills, 18, 22

Private prosecutions, 4

Privilege, 58, 120

Privy Council, 39

Probation, 93

Procedure
civil, 57–62
criminal, 67–68

Prohibition, 37, 61, 113, 119

Prohibitory decisions, 56

Proof, 61, 79

Property, protected, 85

Prosecution, 4, 65

Protests, 128–29

Psychiatric treatment, 89–90

Public administration, 86

Public decency, 86

Public health, 86

Public order, 85

Punishment, 85–94
See also Sentencing
adjournments, 92–93
bonds, 92
changing approach to, 85–86, 94
children, 3, 87–88, 93
corporal, 91
death penalty, 88
deterrence, 87, 89
fines, 91–92
imprisonment, 87, 88–94
insanity, 89–90

parole, 93
penalties, 47, 87
periodic detention, 90
probation, 93
psychiatric treatment, 89–90
purposes, 85–88
reform, 87–88
suspended sentences, 92
youth training centres, 91
work orders, 90
work release, 90

Queen's Counsel, 6, 38, 49, 50, 67

Quo warranto, 56

Racial discrimination, 86
Railways, 43
Re-examination, 60, 71
Reform of offenders, 87–88
Regulations, 140
Remand, 65–66, 111
Remedies, 113–14
Replies, 58, 59
Representation of the parties, 59
Reserved judgments, 111
Reversing decisions, 40
Right to silence, 64–65
Riot, 85
Road accidents, 58, 119, 120
Royal Assent, 8, 15, 22
Royal Commissions, 106, 131
Rules,
    legal system, outside the, 3–4
    unincorporated associations, 3

Sale of goods, 115–16
Scotland
    Court of Session, 39, 40
Search warrants, 64
Secretaries of State, 3, 13–14
Seizure of goods, 61

Self-defence, 86
Self-help, 52–53
Self-incrimination, 115
Sentencing
    See also Punishment
    difficulty, 93
    disparities, 47
    suspended, 92
Separation of powers, 101
Serious fraud, 82
Service of process, 57
Settlement, 54, 99, 110
Silence, right to, 64–65
Solicitors, 49
Sources of law, 5–10
Sovereignty, 15, 141, 149
Specialisation, 49–50, 124
Standard of proof, 61
Statements of claim, 57, 58, 59
Statute law, 8–9
    See also Statutory
    interpretation
    amendment, 12, 19, 27–28
    Cabinet, role of, 21
    common law, affected by, 115–16
    deferred operation, 21–22
    drafting, 19, 26
    effectiveness, 18
    electors, minimal role, 18–19
    entry into force, 22
    European Union, 140
    finding, 12
    gap in, 29
    Government, 104
    House of Lords, 13, 20–21, 102
    making, 9
    non-use, 4
    origins, 17–18
    outmoded, 18
    Parliamentary parties, 19–20, 45, 103
    procedure, 20, 21–22
    Royal Assent, 8, 15, 22
    timing of Bills, 21–22
Statutory instruments, 9

Statutory interpretation, 23–31
  absurdity, 28
  amendments, 27–28
  changing circumstances, 25
  definitions, 27
  drafting in urgency, 26
  failure to use word in same sense, 27
  general terms applied to
    specific circumstances, 28
  Hansard, 30
  inadequate instructions, 25
  injustice, 28
  intention, 25, 29, 30
  judges, 29, 95
  language, 24
  need, 23–24
  reformers, 30
  revising legislation, 26
  role, 28
  rules, 30–31
  technical knowledge, 26
  universally accepted
    meanings, 24–25

Stipendiary magistrates, 5

Strict liability
  criminal, 63–64

Striking out, 55

Subordinate law-
  making bodies, 107–08

Subordinate legislation, 9–10, 12, 33–36
  advantages, 33
  challenging, 35
  change and the law, 130
  delegation of power, 33–35
  difficulties in producing
    effective, 107–08
  disadvantages, 34
  effectiveness, 47, 107–08
  European Union, 140
  judges, 35
  limitations, 107–08
  members of Parliament, 34
  ministerial responsibility, 34
  nature, 33
  Parliament, 45

reasons, 33–34
  supervision, 35
Summary trials, 66
Summons, 57
Superior courts, 6, 9, 11, 38, 57
Sureties, 66
Suspended sentences, 92
Suspects' rights, 64

Technicalities, 113–14
Test of law, 3
Textbooks, 6–7
Time limits, 109
Town planning, 38
Treaties, 139–40, 143–46
Tribunals, 6, 37, 42, 54, 123

Undertakings, 62
Unincorporated associations, 3, 113
Urgent hearings, 55, 96, 113

Vandalism, 90
Vexatious litigants, 3–4
Voting, 45, 146–47, 149

Warrants, 64
Without prejudice, 77
Witnesses, 60
  conflicts between, 112
  experts, 60–61
  intimidating, 65
  judges examining, 60–61, 98
  refreshing memory of, 76–77
Work orders, 90
Work release, 90
Writs, 56, 57

Youth training centres, 91